Companion Planting: The Beginner's Guide to Companion Gardening

Written by M. Grande

This book contains material protected under International and Federal Copyright Laws and Treaties. Any unauthorized reprint or use of this material is prohibited. No part of this book may be reproduced or transmitted in any form or by any means, electronic or mechanical, including photocopying, recording, or by any information storage and retrieval system without express written permission from the author.

© 2014 All rights reserved.

Book 1 of **The Organic Gardening Series** of Books

Disclaimer:

The information contained in this book is for general information purposes only.

While we endeavor to keep the information up to date and correct, we make no representations or warranties of any kind, express or implied, about the completeness, accuracy, reliability, suitability or availability with respect to the book or the information, products, services, or related graphics contained in the book for any purpose. Any reliance you place on such information is therefore strictly at your own risk.

None of the information in this this book is meant to be construed as medical advice. Always consult with a medical profession prior to making any dietary changes in your life.

This book is about fermented beverages. The author of the book is not a trained professional in food safety or any related field. Neither the author nor the publisher is responsible for any damages arising from the use or misuse of the information provided in this book.

Contents

What Is Companion Planting? 8
How Are Good Companions Discovered? 11
The Benefits of Companion Planting 13
Organic Gardening & Companion Planting 15
Companion Planting Strategies 17
Full Sun vs. Partial Shade 19
Allelopathy 22
Insects: The Good & the Bad 24
    Beneficial Insects in the Garden 27
        Damsel Bugs 28
        Hoverflies 29
        Green Lacewings 30
        Ladybugs 31
        Mealybug Destroyer 32
        Nematodes 33
        Parasitic Wasps 34
        Pollinators 35
        Praying Mantis 37
        Predatory Bugs 38
        Spiders 39
        Tachinid Flies 40
    Common Pest Insects 41

  Aphids 42

  Asparagus Beetles 44

  Cabbage worms and Cabbage Loopers 45

  Caterpillars 46

  Colorado Potato Beetle 47

  Flea Beetles 48

  Mealybugs 49

  Mexican Bean Beetle 50

  Japanese Beetles 51

  Scales 52

  Thrips 53

  Tomato Fruitworms (Corn Earworms) 54

  Tomato Hornworm 55

Planning Your Garden 56

Companion Plants 58

  Alfalfa 59

  Almonds 61

  Anise 63

  Apples 64

  Apricots 65

  Asparagus 67

  Asters 69

  Basil 70

  Bay 72

Beets 73

Blueberries 75

Blackberries 77

Borage 79

Broccoli 80

Brussels Sprouts 82

Buckwheat 84

Bush Beans 85

Cabbage 87

Cantaloupe 89

Carrots 91

Catnip 93

Cauliflower 94

Celery 96

Chamomile 98

Chives 100

Clover 102

Coriander (Cilantro) 103

Corn 104

Cranberries 106

Cucumbers 107

Dill 109

Eggplant 111

Fennel 113

Garlic	114
Geraniums	115
Grapes	117
Hyssop	119
Kale	120
Kohlrabi	121
Lavender	123
Leeks	125
Lemon Balm	126
Lettuce	128
Marigolds	130
Mint	132
Mustard	134
Nasturtiums	136
Onions	137
Oregano	139
Parsley	140
Parsnips	142
Peas	144
Peppers	146
Pole Beans	148
Potatoes	150
Pumpkins	152
Radishes	153

- Raspberries 155
- Rhubarb 157
- Rosemary 158
- Roses 159
- Rue 160
- Sage 161
- Spinach 162
- Squash 163
- Stinging Nettles 165
- Strawberries 166
- Sunflowers 168
- Tansy 169
- Thyme 170
- Tomatoes 171
- Turnips 173
- Watermelons 175
- Walnuts, Black 177

Additional Reading 178

What Is Companion Planting?

In life, there are certain people who make better companions than others. Sometimes it's because they share similar interests and are willing to work together toward the same goal and other times it's because they have different interests that are complimentary to one another. For whatever reason, these people are compatible and make a good couple. On the flip side of the coin, there are people who are incompatible and can't even be in the same room without ruffling one another's feathers.

Plants are similar to people in this regard.

Some plants are compatible with one another and have traits that make them great partners, while other plants are incompatible and will battle one another incessantly, leaving both plants exhausted and weak. Knowing which plants are good neighbors and which should be kept away from each other is what companion planting is all about. By carefully choosing neighbors in your garden, you give your seedlings the best possible shot at maturing into happy and healthy plants.

To put it simply, **companion planting** is about plants being planted in close proximity because they're able to help the plants around them out. This could be through nutrients one plant adds to the soil that another plant needs. It could be through insects a plant attracts that help its neighbors or it could be because a plant emits chemicals or has a scent that keeps pests at bay. It could even be something as simple as a taller plant providing shade during the heat of day.

Good companions help the plants around them. Sometimes it's one-sided, as is the case when trap plants are placed in the garden to lure insects away from desirable crops. Other times, the plants mutually benefit one another, like when a plant provides shade to a smaller plant and is rewarded with nutrients being added to the soil.

Regard of the reason, companion planting is your way of mimicking the symbiotic relationships found in nature that occur between different varieties of plants. When you look at an area where plants are growing wild, you won't find them divided neatly by variety. Plants in nature don't grow in the tidy rows found in most gardens. What you'll find in nature is a wide variety of plants, animals and insects living in harmony in a diverse and entirely self-sustainable ecosystem. From the outside looking in, the arrangement of plants in nature looks like chaos, but the reality is it's controlled chaos. Plants have adapted over time to help themselves while taking advantage of the benefits bestowed upon them by other nearby plants.

Companion planting allows you to take *full advantage* of these natural interactions between plants. Blackberries can be used to draw in parasitic wasps that prey on garden pests that eat other plants. Clover and legumes can be used to fix nitrogen into the soil. Asparagus repels nematodes that attack tomatoes. Knowing what each plant in your garden is capable of allows you to create a master plan where each and every plant is placed in a position where it's more likely to thrive because it has neighbors that complement its abilities.

In addition to knowing what plants are good neighbors, it's every bit as important to ensure plants that are bad neighbors are kept on opposite ends of the garden. A person who doesn't know black walnut trees release a chemical that prevents other plants from growing wherever its roots spread may try to grow crop after crop near a walnut tree and fail miserably. Likewise, a person who doesn't understand companion planting may plant a number of Brassica plants close to one another without realizing they're creating a giant beacon in their garden that's calling out to every pest in the neighborhood. An understanding of companion planting and a few tweaks to their plans and both of these individuals would have had successful gardens instead of a constant source of headaches.

If you've been gardening without taking companion planting into consideration, you've been doing it all wrong. Make life much easier on yourself by making life easier on your plants.

How Are Good Companions Discovered?

As you read through this book, you may find yourself wondering where the information on companion planting came from. While certain aspects of companion planting are backed by scientific evidence, much of it is common knowledge that's been handed down from generation to generation and has been proven to work by both gardeners and farmers alike. Our ancient ancestors didn't know why certain plants were good companions. They just were. That didn't stop them from taking advantage of the abilities of their plants.

Farmers and gardeners have known for centuries that certain plants work well together and others don't. They didn't always understand why, as that's something science is just now figuring out, but they knew they were good companions. They figured out which plants grew best together through trial-and-error and passed that information on to their kin. A vast amount of knowledge was built up over the course of many lifetimes. They didn't have companion planting guides to help them along back then. They did it all on their own and in doing so founded much of the information modern companion planting is based upon.

The information in this book is intended to guide you in the right direction, but it's important to realize what works in one garden might not be ideal for another. Each individual garden is its own entity and may have strengths and weaknesses other gardens don't have. It's up to you to discover what works best in your garden.

While the information in this book should point you in the right direction, don't be afraid to experiment and see what works best for you. Spend any amount of time researching good and bad companions and you'll come across recommendations that starkly contrast each other. Some sources say corn and tomatoes are good neighbors, while others say they need to be kept far apart. This difference is more than likely based on personal experience and neither source is incorrect. The reality probably lies somewhere in the middle, with the pair working as companions in gardens where there aren't many of the worms that corn attracts, while they're bad to have together in gardens with a strong worm population.

The best advice I can give is to try companions that look appealing out to see if they work well together. If they do, great. If not, move on to other companions to see if they work better. The only steadfast rule when it comes to companion planting is there are no steadfast rules. There are general guidelines to be aware of, but it's up to the individual to determine what works best in their garden.

The Benefits of Companion Planting

The basic objective of companion planting is to sow plants in close proximity to one another that will benefit their neighbors. Like a neighbor who sees your lawn is getting too long when you've been working long hours and mows it for you, companion plants provide a helping hand the plants that live nearby. Sometimes it's a single direct benefit from one plant to another, while other times the plants are mutually beneficial.

Here are just some of the many ways companion plants can provide a helping hand:

- **They can provide shade.** Sun-sensitive plants can be planted beneath larger plants with broad leaves that provide a protective canopy. Larger plants can be used to filter sunlight and provide dappled light to plants that would otherwise get scorched by the heat of the sun.
- **They can provide nutrients.** Some plants contain large amounts of nutrients other plants need and can be turned into the soil in order to provide successive crops those nutrients. Others add nutrients to the soil as they grow.
- **They make efficient use of garden space.** An example of this would be planting a plant that grows up a trellis in close proximity to a plant that grows along the ground in order to make good use of both horizontal and vertical space. Corn can be planted with beans and the beans can be trained to grow up the corn stalks.

- **They can reduce the amount of maintenance a garden needs.** Planting companion plants that choke out weeds, reduce pests and alleviate disease will make the job of the gardener much easier in the long run. This is especially true with organic gardens because companion plants are often the first and only line of defense.
- **They attract or repel insects.** Some plants attract insects that are beneficial to other plants. Others repel pests.
- **Plants with deep roots can be planted close to plants with shallow root systems.** This allows you to sow plants closer together without having to worry about them competing for water and nutrients.

The best companions fill gaps in the needs of the plants around them. As an example, carrots are susceptible to carrot flies, which are small flies that can sense carrots from up to a mile away. When they find a carrot patch, they'll lay eggs that hatch into maggots that burrow through the roots of the carrot plant and can decimate a crop. The worst part about the carrot fly is you might not know you've been attacked until you go to harvest your carrots and find a bunch of little holes in them. Planting carrots between rows of onions or leeks can confuse the carrot fly and prevent it from picking up the scent of your carrots.

Organic Gardening & Companion Planting

The key to gathering the biggest and best harvests from any garden is making sure plants have the best possible companions. This is especially true for the organic gardener, who doesn't have chemical herbicides and pesticides at their disposal. While traditional gardeners can run down to the local garden center at the first sign of trouble and pick up a chemical cocktail that immediately eliminates most problems that arise, organic gardeners don't have the same tools at their disposal.

Herbicides and pesticides might be the easy way out of trouble, but the organic gardener can rest easy knowing they're growing healthy foods that are largely free of chemicals. Trace amounts of the chemicals used in a garden will make it through to final product. Any pesticide or herbicide (or both) that was used while growing a crop will make it into produce that's harvested from the crop. In the grand scheme of things, a couple tainted pieces of fruit or vegetables aren't going to do much harm, but the cumulative effect of consuming tainted produce daily might.

The understanding that the gardener is going to end up eating a small amount of pretty much everything he treats his or her plants with is the driving factor behind large numbers of gardeners deciding to go organic. While there are obvious health benefits to going organic, it makes gardening a much more difficult proposition.

One of the biggest problems organic gardeners have is weed and pest control. When done right, companion planting can be implemented in organic gardens to prevent pests from ever entering the garden. The pests that do enter are quickly wiped out by predatory insects looking for a quick snack.

You're planting an organic crop that will help out another organic crop. How's that for a green solution?

Companion Planting Strategies

Companion planting can be used in a number of ways in the garden. Every time you turn around, it seems someone is coming up with a new way to use companion plants to their benefit.

Here are just some of the many companion planting strategies that can be employed to help gardeners get the most from their crops:

- **Complimentary planting.** The act of planting two plants close to one another that will bestow benefits upon each other.
- **Cover crops.** These are crops planted to act as ground cover or living mulch. Planting cover crops at the end of gardening season will prevent soil erosion, decrease the impact of water runoff during the rainy season and add organic material to the soil when the cover crop is turned under. Choosing the right type of cover crop is key to ensuring a plot of land continues producing well into the future.
- **Nutrition planting.** Some plants fix certain nutrients into the soil as they grow. Others release nutrients into the soil after they die. Nutrition planting places plants nearby that are ready to take full advantage of the nutrients being released into the soil.
- **Succession planting.** This is a spin on nutrition planting in which plants that benefit one another are planted one after another. For example, bush

beans fix nitrogen into the soil. Corn needs nitrogen to grow. Grow bush beans early in the season and turn them into the soil after harvest. Plant corn in the same area to take full advantage of the nitrogen released into the soil.

- **Pattern disruption.** Plant row after row of similar crops and a single plant infested with pests or disease can spell doom for the rest of your crop as the next plant is only a short hop away. Break plants up by adding other plants between them that aren't susceptible to the same pests and diseases and you've just made it a lot harder for them to spread.
- **Square-foot gardening.** Divide a small garden into 4' X 4' planting areas and divide those areas into plots of 1 square foot apiece and you've got a square-foot garden. Companion plants are important in square-foot gardens because you're trying to grow a lot of plants in a limited amount of space.

A plant that benefits a nearby plant is good. A plant that benefits multiple nearby plants while benefitting from them is even better. The best companions bestow multiple benefits upon one another and are mutually beneficial. Finding a group of plants that all benefit each other in multiple ways is one of the best ways to ensure you have a bumper crop.

Full Sun vs. Partial Shade

One of the biggest decisions you're going to have to make is whether you're going to grow a full sun or a partial shade garden. If you're limited on space, this decision may have already been made for you and you're going to have to work with what you've got. The amount of sun and shade an area gets is one of the major determining factors of the types of plants that can be grown there.

Most fruits and vegetables prefer full sun, so if you're looking grow a produce garden, that's the way to go.

That isn't to say they all prefer sitting in the middle of a desert baking in hot sunlight. **Full sun** is defined as at least 6 hours of sunlight per day, while some plants need as many as 8 to 10 hours per day to thrive. Trying to grow plants that require full sun in an area that gets less exposure to the sun than this will be an exercise in frustration. The plants may grow, but yields will be reduced and they'll be more susceptible to attack from pests and disease.

Partial shade or **partial sun** implies a plant needs less sunlight and can get by on 3 to 6 hours of sunlight per day. These plants do best when they're shaded from the sun in the afternoon when it's at its peak. Placing a plant that prefers partial shade or partial sun in an area that gets full sunlight can scorch the plant when temperatures start to climb, causing it to wilt or even die.

Full shade means relatively little sunlight. There may be a small handful of plants you can grow in full shade, but without much light, you're going to be very limited. If you want to plant fruit and vegetables, you're going to have to find another spot.

Most vegetables, fruits and herbs prefer full sunlight. If you have a garden that only gets partial sunlight, you're going to have to select plants that can be grown with only partial sunlight. There isn't a whole lot you can do to increase the amount of sunlight an area gets short of chopping down trees, moving mountains or tearing down buildings. Reflective mulches can be used to reflect sunlight back up to plants, but the effect is minimal.

Lettuce, spinach, radishes and some varieties of strawberries are well-suited to partially-shaded garden areas. Other crops like peas and potatoes will grow in partial shade, but yields will be reduced. To be clear, these plants will still need sunlight to grow—they just don't need as much as some of the needier plants.

Those looking to grow plants that require partial shade in a full sun location have a handful of options at their disposal. For one, you can build a structure that provides shade during certain times of day. It's best to build a shade that provides relief from the afternoon sun, as opposed to one that provides shade in the morning. Afternoon sunlight is hotter and more likely to damage plants than morning sunlight. Another option is to set up latticework through which the sun can shine. Your plants will get sunlight throughout the day, but won't be exposed to the constant heat of the sun. Some plants will do better than others with this technique, so experiment to find out what works best.

You may be wondering what all this has to do with companion planting. There are some plants that grow tall or have large leaves that spread out that can be used to provide shade to smaller plants. The larger plants can be planted as companion plants to smaller plants that need partial shade. Corn, sunflowers, tomatoes and artichokes can all be planted to provide shade for smaller plants. Trellises plants like pole beans and grapes are also a good way to provide **dappled sunlight**, which is light that's filtered through the leaves of the trellised plant.

These larger sun-loving plants can be planted to provide shade for plants like cabbage, broccoli and cauliflower that don't do well when temperatures start to climb as summer approaches. Smaller plants like carrots, cucumbers and lettuce can also benefit from being planted in the shade of a taller plant as long as the taller plants don't surround them and completely block out the sun.

Trees can be used to provide shade, but you have to be careful not to use a variety of tree that's going to grow to great heights and completely block sunlight from reaching your garden. If trees are already present and are providing too much shade, you may be able to top them or prune them back to ensure your garden gets ample sunlight.

Allelopathy

Allelopathy is defined as the ability of plants to affect other plants through chemical interactions. Biochemicals released by certain plants can have an impact on the growth, survival rate and ability to thrive of plants that attempt to grow within a certain radius of the chemicals. When this effect is beneficial it's known as **positive allelopathy** and when the impact is detrimental it's known as **negative allelopathy**.

While it's been common knowledge for many years that certain plants grow better around certain types of plants and that there are predatory plants around which other plants aren't able to grow, scientists are just now beginning to unlock the reasons why. Cell division, nutrient uptake, photosynthesis and amino acid metabolism are all areas that can be affected by allelopathic chemicals. These chemicals can be released into the soil by the roots of the allelopathic plant or they can be secreted into the air.

Some plants have a much stronger effect on their neighbors than others.

Perhaps the most well-known negative allelopathy comes from the black walnut tree, which releases a chemical into the soil that prevents other plants and trees from growing around them in a radius that can span up to 80' from the tree. Eucalyptus trees, other walnut trees and cottonwood trees can have a similar effect on specific crops, as can trees that are grown on black walnut rootstock.

A number of invasive weeds are also strongly allelopathic and can impact plants planted nearby.

If you have plants in your yard that are known to negatively impact the plants you want to grow in your garden, you're going to need to locate your garden as far from these plants as possible. The allelopathic reach of certain trees can extend far beyond its canopy to anywhere the roots have grown. The roots, stems, branches, leaves and even fruit of these trees can negatively impact your garden, so it's important you keep any debris that falls from the tree from making its way into your garden.

A raised garden with a layer of garden fabric at the bottom may allow you to plant crops closer to allelopathic trees than you'd normally be able to. You can also try planting Kentucky bluegrass in the immediate vicinity of the problematic tree because it's one of the few plants that can grow near allelopathic trees and is able to eliminate some of the biochemicals emitted by trees. Discard the clippings when you mow the grass. Don't add these clippings to your compost bin.

Insects: The Good & the Bad

When you plant a garden, you can count on it attracting a vast number of insects. Some will be good, some will be bad and some won't make much of a difference one way or the other. Determine the insects each plant in your garden is likely to attract and plan accordingly. Take note of both the pests and the beneficial insects each plant is likely to attract. Then select complimentary plants that will repel or otherwise eliminate the pests you know are likely to make an appearance.

There are a handful of ways companion planting can benefit your garden when it comes to both attracting and discouraging insects:

- **Some plants repel certain types of pests because they don't care for their look, smell or taste.**
- **Some plants draw in predatory insects that prey on garden pests.**
- **Some plants create a green canopy that makes it tough for pests to identify the plants they want to land on.**
- **Some plants act as "trap plants" that can be planted to draw insects out of your garden.**
- **Some plants have strong scents that mask the scent of other plants that are susceptible to attack.**

In order to understand how beneficial companion planting is to insect control in a garden, let's pretend we're an aphid flying over the average garden. The aphid identifies a patch of green, floats down to the garden and picks a plant. Chances are the plant it lands on is going to be one it likes, as aphids suck sap out of most fruit and vegetable plants. Since aphids are capable of **parthenogenesis**, which is asexual reproduction, a single aphid landing on a plant in your garden could result in millions or even billions of aphids being born over the course of a growing season. The ability of aphids to rapidly reproduce is the reason your garden goes from perfectly fine to completely-infested seemingly overnight. They reproduce, suck sap until the plant they're on starts to dry out and then sprout wings so they can move on to the next plant.

Next, let's picture a garden that's been planted with companion plants designed to keep aphids at bay. The aphid still flies over the garden and identifies it as a potential source of food, but this time moves closer to find the garden is full of onions, garlic, marigolds, coriander, dill and other plants that repel aphids. If it's lucky enough to find a plant far enough away from the scents it doesn't like to be tolerable, it soon finds itself under attack from voracious predators that have been drawn in by the plants in the garden. Ladybugs and green lacewings are roaming the garden, looking for a tasty little aphid to make a meal of. The aphid finds the garden to be a very inhospitable place and either leaves for greener pastures or falls victim to one of the many predators prowling its leaves and branches.

An additional layer of security can be added to the garden in the form of **trap crops**, which are crops designed to draw in pests and keep them in the trap crop, sacrificing a less-desirable crop for one you don't want to get attacked. An example of this would be planting geraniums near rose bushes because Japanese beetles are drawn away from the roses to the geraniums, which then proceed to poison the beetles and kill them off.

Another way companion plants can benefit gardens is by acting as "**green decoys**." The more green there is in a garden, the harder it becomes for pests to identify the plants they want to prey on. Scientific studies have revealed pests are less likely to find plants they want when they're surrounded by less-desirable green plants. In fact, some studies have shown green plastic or green cardboard is an effective decoy that can be used to prevent pests from landing in a garden.

Designing your garden in a manner that drives away pests and makes them less likely to find your money crops will go a long way toward making sure your garden remains healthy. In order to properly plan a garden, you've got to have a good understanding of exactly what predators and beneficial insects will be attracted to it and then take steps to eliminate the bad ones while calling in more of the good ones.

Beneficial Insects in the Garden

Let's take a look at some of the beneficial insects you may be able to attract to your garden and why it's good to have them around. Depending on where you live, you might not be able to attract all of these insects, but should be able to attract enough of them to make a difference.

A local nursery should be able to tell you the insects found in your area. They've probably had to battle all of them at one time or another. Failing that, you may be able to head to a local farmers market and get some good information from the vendors there. Look for farmers selling organic vegetables, as they're usually more in tune with the local insect population. Conventional farmers tend to spray everything, killing all insects in the process.

Damsel Bugs

Damsel bugs are a great predator insect to have around because they don't discriminate come dinnertime and will attempt to eat anything smaller than they are. They enjoy aphids, caterpillars, spider mites and tree hoppers, but will make short work of pretty much anything they happen upon. If you're able to attract these beneficial insects, provide them with some sort of groundcover crop to overwinter in and you'll have damsel bugs in your garden again come springtime.

The following plants attract damsel bugs:

- **Caraway.**
- **Fennel.**
- **Marigold.**
- **Mint.**

Hoverflies

Hoverflies, also known as flower flies, are aptly named because they move their wings so fast they appear to be hovering in the air. These little flies flit and fly around the garden, laying eggs that hatch into maggots that prey on aphids, mealybugs and other pests.

The following plants all attract hoverflies:

- **Buckwheat.**
- **Caraway.**
- **Chamomile.**
- **Coriander.**
- **Dill.**
- **Fennel.**
- **Lavender.**
- **Lemon balm.**
- **Marigolds.**
- **Oregano.**
- **Parsley.**
- **Thyme.**
- **Yarrow.**

Green Lacewings

Adult green lacewings feed primarily on flower nectar. The larvae are the real predators and will attack scales, aphids, thrips and even small caterpillars and moth eggs. If you aren't able to attract lacewings to your garden naturally, lacewing eggs can be ordered online. Spread the eggs out on the plants you want to protect and little larvae affectionately known as "aphid lions" will hatch and terrorize all of the tiny pests they can find.

Lacewings are attracted to the following plant types:

- **Buckwheat.**
- **Caraway.**
- **Catnip.**
- **Dandelions.**
- **Tansy.**

Ladybugs

Don't let the black and white head and cute little black dots on their pretty red shell fool you. Ladybugs are about as voracious a predator as there is when it comes to garden insects. Ladybugs love to dine on aphids and other soft-shelled insects and will quickly clear them out of your garden. Both adult ladybugs and larvae feed on pests, so be careful not to wash the larvae off of your plants when watering them. Water at the base of plants instead of spraying water over the top if you're trying to increase the population of ladybugs in your garden.

The following plants are known to attract ladybugs:

- **Buckwheat.**
- **Coriander.**
- **Dandelions.**
- **Dill.**
- **Fennel.**
- **Lemon balm.**
- **Marigolds.**
- **Sunflowers.**
- **Tansy.**
- **Yarrow.**

Mealybug Destroyer

This is one insect that lives up to its namesake. I'll give you one guess what its favorite meal is...That's right, mealybugs. This intimidating little creature loves mealybugs, but also dines on aphids and other soft-shelled pests.

Attract mealybug destroyers to your garden by planting the following plants:

- **Dill.**
- **Fennel.**
- **Sunflowers.**
- **Tansy.**
- **Yarrow.**

Nematodes

Nematodes are microscopic worm-like creatures that prey on more than 200 different species of pest insects and will consume ants, Japanese beetles, pine beetles and cabbage worms. There are both good and bad nematodes. The bad nematodes feed on plants and will pierce their stems and roots to suck out sap. Good nematodes pierce insects and suck out their juices.

You may have to purchase nematodes if you want them in your garden because they live in the soil and aren't easy to attract. Once you spread them around your garden, keep them there by planting cover crops that protect the soil they live in.

Parasitic Wasps

Don't let the name fool you into thinking these little guys are dangerous. They don't sting humans and the only thing they're a danger to is pests like moths, beetles and caterpillars. Parasitic moths inject their eggs into the bodies of pest insects, which then hatch and consume their host.

The following plants are known to attract parasitic wasps:

- **Anise.**
- **Borage.**
- **Coriander.**
- **Dill.**
- **Fennel.**
- **Lavender.**
- **Lemon balm.**
- **Marigolds.**
- **Mint.**
- **Oregano.**
- **Parsley.**
- **Tansy.**
- **Yarrow.**

Pollinators

The term **pollinator** encompasses a vast number of insects and creatures that transfer pollen from one flower to another. Birds, bees, beetles, butterflies, moths and even bats all fall under the umbrella term "pollinators." These creatures are crucial to have around gardens containing plants with flowers that require pollination in order to bear fruit. They're also a necessity for those looking to collect seeds from plants that require pollination.

Generally speaking, plants that produce brightly-colored flowers will draw in pollinators. If they have a lot of flowers or have large flowers, they'll call in more pollinators than plants with only a few smaller flowers. In order for plants that call in pollinators to be effective, they have to be blooming at the same time the crops you want to pollinate are.

Here are some plants you can grow in your garden to bring pollinators in:

- **Asters.**
- **Basil.**
- **Borage.**
- **Buckwheat.**
- **Catnip.**
- **Chives.**
- **Corn.**
- **Dill.**
- **Fennel.**
- **Geraniums.**
- **Hyssop.**

- Lavender.
- Lemon balm.
- Mint.
- Oregano.
- Parsley.
- Sunflowers.
- Thyme.

Praying Mantis

The praying mantis is a long-lived predator insect that's willing to dine on pretty much any other insect it comes across. Larger mantises have been known to snatch up lizards, frogs and the occasional hummingbird. Barring being eaten by a predator, a mantis can live for as long as a year from the time it hatches. They're great to have in the garden, but rarely stick around for long periods of time.

Mantises are attracted to the following plants:

- **Flowering plants and shrubs.**
- **Pine trees.**
- **Raspberries.**

Predatory Bugs

The term "**predatory bugs**" encompasses a number of small predators, including minute pirate bugs, ambush bugs and assassin bugs. These little bugs prey on aphids, thrips, mites, tomato hornworms, corn earworms and other soft-bodied pests.

Here are some plants that are known to call in predatory bugs:

- **Alfalfa.**
- **Buckwheat.**
- **Clover.**
- **Coriander.**
- **Corn.**
- **Fennel.**
- **Flowers.**
- **Hairy Vetch.**
- **Shrubs.**
- **Tansy.**

Spiders

While they're technically not insects, spiders are predatory creatures that will make short work of any insect unlucky enough to get caught in their web. Garden spiders primarily feed on flying insects that become entangled in their web.

Plant perennial plants with thick foliage in which spiders can set up residence to increase the number of spiders in your garden. As much as it's going to bother you, it's best to avoid disturbing their webs, even when they string them up in inconvenient places.

Tachinid Flies

Tachinid flies act in a manner similar to parasitic wasps. They lay eggs on caterpillars, worms, stink bugs and a number of other beetles and flying insects. The eggs hatch and the larvae proceed to eat the pests from the inside out. It isn't pretty, but it's a great way to eliminate stubborn pests once and for all.

The following plants are known to draw in tachinid flies:

- **Buckwheat.**
- **Lemon balm.**
- **Parsley.**
- **Tansy.**

Common Pest Insects

While the perfect garden would only attract beneficial insects that would prey on anything and everything that dared step foot into the garden, that's rarely the case. Most gardens contain a wide variety of insects, both good and bad.

Let's take a closer look at some of the more common pests found in gardens across the country. If you're lucky, you won't have to deal with more than one or two of these insects at once.

Aphids

Aphids, also known as plant lice, are tiny little insects that can quickly multiply into a huge problem that spans across the vast majority of a garden. A single aphid making its way into an unprotected garden can result in millions or even billions of aphids quickly populating every nook, cranny and corner of your garden.

Aphids can have up to 12 live babies per day. Within the first week, one aphid can have 84 babies. Within a week those aphids are ready to start having babies of their own. The 84 babies will start adding 12 babies apiece per day, which is more than 1,000 aphids being added daily. Once they start having babies, the numbers jump even more dramatically. Within a month, millions of aphids will be infesting the garden. Of course, this simple scenario assumes no aphids die and that each of the aphids has exactly 12 babies per day, but you get the point.

Luckily, you have some options when it comes to controlling aphids. You can plant caraway, chamomile, dandelions, buckwheat and tansy to attract insects that prey on them. Ladybugs, green lacewings, praying mantises and minute pirate bugs will all make a meal of aphids. Nasturtiums can be used as a trap crop for aphids.

Additionally, you can use the following plants to repel aphids:

- **Basil.**
- **Catnip.**
- **Chives.**
- **Clover.**

- **Coriander.**
- **Dill.**
- **Eucalyptus.**
- **Fennel.**
- **Garlic.**
- **Onions.**
- **Nettles.**
- **Peppermint.**
- **Radishes.**

A combination of plants that attract insects that attack aphids and plants that aphids don't care for seems to be the best way to prevent aphids from making their way into the garden. If you catch an infestation while it's underway, use a strong spray of water to wash aphids away from your plants. Watch your plants closely after that and wash them down again if the aphids return.

Asparagus Beetles

Asparagus beetles are orange and white or blue-black beetles that prey on asparagus shoots. From larvae to mature adults, asparagus beetles will make a meal of both the leaves and the stems of the asparagus plant. Knock the larger beetles into a bucket of soap to get rid of them.

Ladybug larvae will eat both the eggs and the larvae of the asparagus beetle, so keep plants that attract ladybugs in your garden. Additionally, the following plants are known to deter asparagus beetles:

- **Basil.**
- **Coriander.**
- **Parsley.**
- **Petunias.**
- **Tomatoes.**

Cabbage worms and Cabbage Loopers

Cabbage worms and cabbage loopers attack Brassica crops all across North America. They look like white or green caterpillars and will tunnel through the roots of cabbages.

Beneficial nematodes are the main predator needed in the garden to clear out cabbage worms. Nematodes will likely have to be purchased because they're difficult to attract. In addition to adding nematodes to the soil, the following plants can be grown to prevent cabbage worms from ever making their way into a garden:

- **Borage.**
- **Celery.**
- **Dill.**
- **Radishes.**
- **Rosemary.**
- **Sage.**
- **Thyme.**
- **Tomatoes.**

Another option is to plant a crop like mustard that attracts cabbage loopers and cabbage worms around the outside of your garden as a trap crop that can be sacrificed to protect more desirable crops.

Caterpillars

Caterpillars attack a wide range of plants, chewing on leaves, tunneling through fruit and leaving droppings behind everywhere they go. While the butterflies some of them will eventually become may be beneficial to a garden, they're quite the pest while in the caterpillar stage. Of particular concern are cutworms and cabbage loopers, which have been known to quickly strip plants of their foliage.

In order to keep caterpillars at bay, add plants to your garden that draw in parasitic wasps, praying mantises and green lacewings. Another option is to hang a bird feeder to call in birds that'll come for the bird food and supplement their meals with any caterpillars that cross their paths. When you see a caterpillar, handpick it and move it far from your garden.

The following plants can be planted in a garden to repel caterpillars:

- **Lavender.**
- **Peppermint.**
- **Sage.**

Colorado Potato Beetle

The Colorado potato beetle looks like a yellowish-orange ladybug with stripes instead of dots. While ladybugs are a preferred predator in the garden and will eat Colorado potato beetles, these pests will quickly defoliate peppers, potatoes, eggplant and tomatoes. In addition to ladybugs, nematodes are beneficial to have around when potato beetles are present.

Some sources indicate the Colorado potato beetle doesn't like to walk over coarse mulch. Adding a layer of straw mulch around your plants may prevent the beetle from making it to your plants.

The following plants will repel Colorado potato beetles:

- **Catnip.**
- **Chives.**
- **Coriander.**
- **Eucalyptus.**
- **Garlic.**
- **Green beans.**
- **Marigolds.**
- **Nasturtiums.**
- **Peas.**

Flea Beetles

These tiny little pests are found across the entirety of North America. They chew small, round holes in the leaves of most vegetables and will jump around nervously when disturbed. Flea beetles prefer dry soil to lay their eggs in, so keep your soil damp to make your garden less attractive. Nematodes can be added to the soil to make short work of any larvae that do hatch.

The following plants will repel flea beetles:

- **Catnip.**
- **Peppermint.**
- **Rue.**
- **Thyme.**

Mealybugs

Mealybugs are tiny creatures that appear in clusters at the base of leaves. They'll attack a wide variety of fruit and vegetables, including citrus trees, grapes and potatoes. They suck sap out of plants and leave a honeydew residue behind that can quickly start to mold.

Lacewings and mealybug destroyers enjoy eating mealybugs, so do what it takes to attract them to your garden. Companion planting isn't an effective means of eliminating mealybugs.

Mexican Bean Beetle

The Mexican bean beetle is a connoisseur of a number of varieties of beans. It has a bottomless pit for a stomach and will continue chewing on the leaves of a plant until it starts to die. These beetles roam the Western half of the United States, looking for bean crops to devastate.

Soybeans can be planted as a trap crop to prevent Mexican bean beetles from reaching your money crops. Plants that draw in soldier bugs are a good bet as well. Another tactic you can employ is laying aluminum foil on the ground around your beans to reflect heat and prevent the beetles from landing.

The following plants are known to repel Mexican bean beetles:

- **Garlic.**
- **Marigolds.**
- **Rosemary.**

Japanese Beetles

Japanese beetles are commonly found in the Eastern half of the United States and are known to attack a variety of vegetables and flowers. They're a bluish-green color and feature rust-colored wing covers. They're pretty to look at, but the damage they can do to a crop is anything but pretty.

Since these beetles are large and easy to see, your best bet may be collecting them by hand and knocking them into a container of soapy water. Nematodes will feed on the grubs, but most natural predators won't eat the beetles themselves.

The following plants will deter Japanese beetles:

- **Catnip.**
- **Chives.**
- **Chrysanthemums.**
- **Garlic.**
- **Marigolds.**
- **Onions.**
- **Rue.**

Scales

Scales are aptly named because, at a glance, they look like small scales attached to a plant. They're destructive little creatures that will suck sap from plants during every stage of their life cycle. When you notice scales on your plants, prune them back to get rid of the affected areas or scrub them off the branches.

There are no plants that are known to deter scales, so you'll have to rely on predatory insects to get the job done. Ladybugs, praying mantises and green lacewings will all dine on scales, so plants that attract them may help.

Thrips

These tiny insects are so small you probably won't see them on your plants. What you will see are discolored areas that take on an almost silvery sheen as the thrips bite into the plants repeatedly and leave a large number of tiny little scars. Thrips aren't problematic unless the population gets out of control and begins to spread viruses. P
lants may wilt and start to turn yellow while under attack from thrips. Keep plants and soil damp if you suspect a thrip attack is underway. Thrips prefer dry conditions and will avoid damp areas. There aren't a whole lot of plants thrips will avoid, but they have been known to steer clear of oregano.

Tomato Fruitworms (Corn Earworms)

Tomato fruitworms, also known as corn earworms, cotton bollworms and geranium budworms, are found in gardens throughout North America. These worms are known by a number of names, usually indicative of the type of plant they're attacking. They've been known to dine on cotton, beans, peas, peppers, tomatoes, corn, geraniums, potatoes and squash.

The adults are small moths that lay eggs on the bottoms of leaves. The larvae feed on the leaves as they grow. If they're attacking a corn crop, they'll move into the husks as the corn matures and will eventually begin to feed on the silk and the corn kernels at the ends of the ears.

Geraniums and thyme are known to deter the tomato fruitworm.

Tomato Hornworm

This large caterpillar is found in gardens throughout the United States, usually munching on the leaves of eggplant, peppers, potatoes and tomatoes. They develop into large moths that have a wingspan of up to 5".

Handpick caterpillars off of your plants and destroy them. Grow plants that attract parasitic moths to clean up any hornworms you miss. When harvesting hornworms by hand, keep an eye out for the tell-tall white eggs attached to the backs of the caterpillars you're collecting. If you see eggs, return them to the garden. The caterpillar is doomed regardless and its death will result in more parasitic wasps.

The following plants will repel tomato hornworms:

- **Borage.**
- **Dill.**
- **Thyme.**

Planning Your Garden

The key to successful companion planting is properly planning where the plants in your garden are going to go. You've got to carefully consider how each of the plants in your garden are going to interact with one another and then place them in the best possible locations to take advantage of those interactions. The biggest limitation in regard to companion planting is the knowledge of the gardener. Arm yourself with as much knowledge as possible before you ever put on your gardening gloves.

The first step to proper garden planning is deciding which plants you want in your garden. Create a master list of the plants you absolutely need to have and plan your garden around that list. Once you have a list of essential plants, supplement the list with a handful of other plants you wouldn't mind having.

Now, get to work researching the potential interactions between the plants you need and the plants you'd like to have. Consider allelopathy, pests, beneficial insects, the heights of the plants and the depths of the root systems to create groupings of plants that will work hand-in-hand. Plants that are beneficial to one another should be kept together, while plants that are detrimental to each other should be planted at opposite ends of the garden.

Once you've got your garden planned, take a closer look at the plants you've included in the plans and see if there are any other plants you didn't include that can help. Flowers, ground cover and other smaller good neighbors may be able to be squeezed into small areas of the garden to good effect. With companion planting, you aren't going to have your typical garden with row after orderly row of produce. Instead, you're going have plants that are mixed and matched because of what they can do for one another.

Don't start planting until you've got your garden mapped out. It's the best way to ensure you keep good neighbors together and bad neighbors far apart.

Companion Plants

Alfalfa

Alfalfa is primarily grown as a forage crop because it's easy to grow and is a high-value feed crop that's high in protein. It prefers deep, well-drained soil, but can be grown in a wide variety of soil types. Alfalfa sprouts can be consumed by humans, but the full-grown plants are generally used for animal feed.

As far as the home garden is concerned, alfalfa is generally planted as a cover crop that can be grown between crops that place a heavy load on the soil. Plant your garden with alfalfa and turn it into the soil and you'll ensure successive gardens have the nutrients they need to successfully grow.

Another use for alfalfa is as ground cover that can be planted between garden crops. When planted as cover, alfalfa can prevent weed growth and will confuse pests looking for a green plant to land on. Alfalfa benefits cotton plants by attracting insects that prey on the pests that attack cotton. Corn is a good neighbor to alfalfa because it spreads out and provides shade to the root systems of the corn while driving away pests and adding nutrients to the soil. The root system of corn is shallower than that of alfalfa, which means there won't be much competition between the two.

If you've got hard pan or thick clay soil, alfalfa can be used to break up the soil. It has a deep rooting system and has even been known to push roots through rocks. Avoid planting alfalfa around tomatoes because it has been shown to be allelopathic toward tomato seedlings.

Good Neighbors:

Corn, cotton, most other plants.

Bad Neighbors:
Tomatoes.

Known Benefits:
Alfalfa increases the level of iron, magnesium, nitrogen, phosphorous and potassium in the soil. It can also be planted to increase the amount of green foliage in the garden in order to confuse pests looking to land on something green. Additionally, alfalfa crops can be planted to provide habitat for predatory and parasitic insects that will prey on pests.

Almonds

If you live in a climate warm enough to grow almonds, consider yourself very lucky. It can take up to 5 years for young trees to start producing, but once they do you'll be able to harvest almonds from them annually for up to 50 years. A single healthy, full-grown tree can produce upwards of 40 pounds of almonds per year.

Be careful when picking the variety of almond tree you want to grow. If you're looking for edible almonds similar to the ones found on store shelves, sweet almonds are the way to go. Ornamental and flowering almond trees are largely ornamental and won't produce much by way of almonds. Bitter almond trees produce almonds, but they contain cyanide and are strongly astringent.

The most important companion tree for almond trees that aren't of the self-pollinating variety is to plant other almond trees nearby. This improves the rate of pollination and helps ensure the fruits that contain the nuts will form. If the flowers don't get pollinated, the fruits won't develop and there won't be any almonds come harvest time.

Almond trees are good to plant around blackberries because they hold moisture in their canopies and drop leaves that turn into mulch.

Good Neighbors:
Blackberries, chives, garlic.

Bad Neighbors:
Plants that require full sunlight won't do well around established almond trees with thick canopies.

Known Benefits:

Almonds can hold moisture in their leaves. When the leaves fall they turn into natural organic mulch.

Anise

Anise is a strong-scented herb that has the flavor of licorice. It grows tall, so it can be used to provide shade for low-growing plants. It's said to improve the vigor of any plant grown in close proximity and is a popular choice for flower beds.

Coriander especially benefits from being grown near anise because it speeds up germination. Broccoli and other Brassica family plants benefit from anise because it masks their smell, preventing pests that target their scents.

Good Neighbors:
Beans, Brassica family plants, coriander.

Bad Neighbors:
Carrots, rue.

Known Benefits:
Anise is known to deter lice and some biting insects, while attracting predatory wasps that prey on aphids. The strong scent of anise masks the scent of nearby plants, hiding them from pests.

Apples

Apple trees are a great addition to most backyards. They run the gamut from huge trees that reach more than 25' in height to smaller dwarf or hedge varieties that only grow to 8' to 10' tall, so there's an apple tree for almost any yard. Apple trees can be grown in containers, so you may even be able to grow apples if all you have is a concrete patio.

Chives are good neighbors to apple trees because they help ward off apple scab. Onions and garlic are good neighbors because they ward off a variety of pests. Nasturtium wards off the codling moth, but may be ineffective on larger trees. Black walnut trees are bad neighbors because they can inhibit the growth of apple trees. Cedar trees should also be avoided because they can spread apple-cedar rust to apple trees that are planted nearby.

Good Neighbors:
Borage, catnip, chives, garlic, leeks, nasturtium, onions, parsley, parsnips.

Bad Neighbors:
Cedar trees, walnuts.

Known Benefits:
No known benefits.

Apricots

Many apricot varieties are early bloomers and may not be a good choice for areas that get late frosts because a good frost can kill the bloom. When choosing a variety, carefully consider whether you want an early-, midseason- or late-blooming tree. If you live in an area prone to late frosts, choose a variety that blooms later in the year. If you live in a warmer climate and frost isn't of concern you can plant the early bloomers as well as the late bloomers. In areas where the climate is perfect for apricots, you may be able to plant all three and have a staggered harvest throughout the summer.

Apricot trees can reach 30' in height and a single tree can produce up to 100 pounds of apricots. Apricot trees can live up to 70 years.

Peppers can pass a fungus on to apricots that does a significant amount of damage, so don't plant peppers anywhere near your apricot trees. Tomatoes, eggplant and potatoes can also pass diseases on to apricots.

Basil is a good choice to plant near apricots, as long as you live in a warm enough zone for it to grow. Basil plants repel many of the insects that prey on apricots. Trim any flower buds that develop in the basil back as soon as they form in order to keep the aroma of the basil strong enough to ward off insects. Garlic is another good neighbor because it repels aphids and tree borers, with the added bonus of keeping moles at bay.

Good Neighbors:
Basil, borage, catnip, chives, garlic, parsnips.

Bad Neighbors:
Eggplant, peppers, potatoes, tomatoes.

Known Benefits:
No known benefits.

Asparagus

Asparagus is a dinner-time favorite that tastes equally great whether lightly oiled and tossed on the grill, boiled or steamed. Asparagus stalks can grow to heights of 5' or more, but are rarely allowed to do so because they become woody and inedible. Harvest asparagus for eating when it's around 8" to 10" in height.

This hardy plant is good neighbors with a number of plants and gets along well with most neighbors. When paired with basil, it's believed to draw in ladybugs that keep aphids out of the garden. Comfrey is a good choice because it dies back as the asparagus starts to grow and will provide food for the growing asparagus plants. Just be aware that comfrey can grow out of control and may need to be cut back in order to give asparagus space.

Planting tomatoes in close proximity to asparagus will help deter asparagus beetles. Asparagus returns the favor by deterring nematodes that attack the tomatoes. Coriander and dill will also help deter some pests that attack asparagus plants. Pot marigolds are another plant that can be planted in rows with asparagus in order to deter beetles. If harmful nematodes are a problem, asters can be planted to drive them away.

Since asparagus stalks are thin when they're young, there's a lot of room for weed growth between the stalks. Planting a bushy plant like strawberries close to asparagus works well because strawberry plants will spread out to fill up open space, choking out much of the weed growth.

Good Neighbors:

Asters, basil, cabbage, comfrey, coriander, dill, marigolds, parsley, peas, strawberries, tomatoes.

Bad Neighbors:
Broccoli, chives, garlic, onions, potatoes.

Known Benefits:
Asparagus can be planted around low-growing plants and will provide mottled shade for the plants during the heat of the day. Planting asparagus near tomato plants will help repel the nematodes that attack tomatoes.

Asters

This brightly-colored flower blooms well into the late summer and fall and can add color to a garden long after most summer blooms have lost their luster. Asters range from small in stature at 6" to 8" to very tall, with some varieties reaching heights approaching 8'.

While asters are compatible with most vegetables, they need to be kept away from celery and corn because they're carriers of aster yellows disease, which can cause deformities in the flowers of the aster plant. Asparagus thrives when planted near asters because they repel harmful nematodes and a handful of other insects.

Good Neighbors:
Asparagus, most vegetables.

Bad Neighbors:
Carrots, celery, corn.

Known Benefits:
Attracts pollinating insects and ladybugs, while repelling nematodes and other insects.

Basil

Basil is a bushy annual garden herb that can grow up to 2' tall. It's a highly fragrant plant used in a wide variety of dishes as a seasoning herb.

Basil is beneficial when planted near most garden crops, as it aids with growth and repels a number of insects. When paired with asparagus, basil is thought to draw ladybugs into the garden. When planted in close proximity to tomatoes, both plants end up tasting better.

Basil helps tomatoes grow like crazy and benefits from having tomatoes nearby. Peppers realize a similar benefit from basil. There are conflicting reports on what happens when you grow basil and anise close to one another. Some sources say they're good companions, while other sources say they shouldn't be planted near one another.

An added bonus of planting basil in your garden is its ability to deter mosquitoes and flies. Keep a container of basil close to where people congregate and you'll reduce the number of flying pests you have to deal with, both in the garden and while hanging out in your backyard on a Saturday afternoon.

Good Neighbors:
Apricots, asparagus, broccoli, grapes, nettles, peppers, roses, strawberries, tomatoes.

Bad Neighbors:
Rue, sage.

Known Benefits:

Basil helps deter fungal growth and is capable of driving away a number of insects, including aphids, asparagus beetles, mites and mosquitoes. In addition to driving away bad insects, basil also attracts butterflies, which can aid with pollination.

Bay

Bay leaves come from the bay laurel tree, which is an evergreen tree native to Greece. It prefers a moderate climate and doesn't do well in areas that experience deep freezes. Bay can be grown in containers, so that may be an option for those looking to grow bay in a cooler climate.

Be careful when choosing a variety of bay to grow because some varieties have leaves that are toxic. As long as you're sure your bay is safe to eat, bay leaves can be harvested from your tree(s) any time of the year. Bay leaves need to be dried before use because otherwise they'll be bitter.

Good Neighbors:
Most plants can be grown near bay laurel trees.

Bad Neighbors:
No known bad neighbors, but bay laurel trees may compete with nearby plants for nutrients in the soil.

Known Benefits:
Bay leaves will deter weevils and moths. This effect is more pronounced when bay leaves are dried and crushed and dispersed into the soil.

Beets

Beets are a cool season crop that grows rapidly and is able to withstand near-freezing temperatures. It's a good choice to plant close to the end of the harvest season and is a favorite amongst the Northern gardeners who only have a small handful of plants they can grow in the cool climate.

Plant garlic or mint nearby for more robust beet plants. Garlic wards off maggots, beetles and snails that attack the beets and people who plant them together often claim the flavor of both plants is enhanced. Mint keeps beetles and fleas away, while attracting predatory wasps that prey on aphids. The strong scent of mint may even prevent some larger animals from coming close. One concern with planting mint nearby is it grows quickly and is an invasive plant. A better option is to grow mint in a container and add mint leaf clippings to the ground around your beets.

Beets benefit from having bush beans nearby, but need to be kept away from pole beans. When beets are planted in close proximity to pole beans, both plants may end up with stunted growth, so be sure to leave plenty of distance between pole beans and beets. Avoid planting beets near plants that grow to tall heights, as they will outcompete beets for light and will block them from getting the light they need to thrive. Avoid corn, squash, watermelon, sunflowers and tomatoes for this reason. Mustard is another bad neighbor because it emits a chemical that can slow the growth of beets.

Kohlrabi and beets are good plants to have as neighbors because they're similar enough to feed, water and care for in a similar manner, but their root systems reach different levels of the soil. Kohlrabi has shallow roots, while beets dig a little deeper to meet their nutritional needs. Onions are also good neighbors to beets.

Good Neighbors:
Broccoli, Brussels sprouts, bush beans, cabbage, catnip, cauliflower, cucumbers, garlic, lettuce, kale, kohlrabi, mint, onions.

Bad Neighbors:
Corn, mustard, pole beans, squash, sunflowers, tomatoes, watermelon.

Known Benefits:
Beets add minerals to the soil, namely magnesium. This benefits a number of vegetables, but members of the cabbage family benefit most. Cabbage, kale, broccoli, kohlrabi, Brussels sprouts and cauliflower are all plants that benefit from having beets nearby.

Blueberries

There are 4 basic types of blueberry plants and the type you choose may mean the difference between having plenty of blueberries come harvest time and having nothing but trouble.

Here's a quick rundown of all 4 types:

- **Highbush blueberries** are the type you see sold in supermarkets and are aptly named because they can grow to 8' in height. Northern highbush blueberries are more frost-tolerant than southern highbush blueberries, which do best in warmer climates.
- **Lowbush blueberries** are much shorter than highbush blueberries, rarely reaching more than 2' in height. Their squat stature allows them to be able to be grown in climates where winter temperatures fall below freezing.
- **Rabbiteye blueberries** usually fall somewhere between lowbush and highbush blueberries in height and are a good option for southern gardeners in warm climates.
- **Half-high blueberries** are about half the height of highbush blueberries, but still feature the large, juicy berries characteristic of the larger plants. These berries are able to be grown in cooler regions than highbush berries, but aren't as cold-hardy as lowbush berries.

Blueberries require strongly acidic soil, so there aren't a whole lot of plants that can successfully be paired up with them. If you've got pine or oak trees on your property, they create acidic soil and blackberries will usually do well when planted nearby. Blackberries are one of the few plants able to handle the acidic pH required by blueberries and are good neighbors, but the yield of the blackberries may take a hit due to the acidity of the soil. Cranberries, raspberries and rhubarb also prefer acidic soil and can be grown with blueberries.

One of the best companion plants you can provide for your blueberry bushes is another blueberry bush of another variety. When cross-pollination occurs, blueberries on both bushes will be bigger and the yield will improve.

Good Neighbors:
Blackberries, cranberries, pine trees, oak trees, raspberries, rhubarb, strawberries.

Bad Neighbors:
Plants that can't handle acidic soil.

Known Benefits:
No known benefits.

Blackberries

If you live in a climate conducive to blackberry growth and have room in your yard, a blackberry bush or two will provide you up to 10 pounds of tasty berries per plant per growing season. Erect and semi-trailing plants need 4' between plants, while trailing blackberries need at least 6'. Early-, mid- and late-season harvest varieties are available. Selecting at least one of each will ensure you have berries available throughout the growing season.

While most people think of unruly bushes growing in the wild when they think of blackberries, it's possible to trellis blackberry bushes to make them more manageable. Trellised berries will provide easy access to all of the berries, which is especially important if you're growing one of the thorned varieties.

Blackberries prefer full sun, but can be planted below trees with large canopies as a complimentary plant. The yields will be reduced, but the blackberries will benefit from the leaves that are dropped and the moisture that's retained by the canopy. Almond, oak, cherry and pear trees are all good companions to blackberries.

A variety of ground cover plants can be planted around blackberries. Chives, lemon balm and mint all benefit blackberries because they can be planted close enough to their bare stems to protect them from insect attack and they attract pollinating insects. Strawberries extend the harvest of blackberries while also providing ground cover.

The nitrogen needs of blackberry bushes are high. Peas and beans work well as companions in this regard because they fix nitrogen into the soil. Cut bean plants off near the ground once they begin to slow instead of attempting to pull them because you can damage the intertangled roots of nearby blackberries.

Blueberries prefer highly acidic soil, so there aren't many plants that can be paired up with them. Blackberries are able to tolerate the acidic soil required for growing blueberries and make good neighbors. Be aware the yield of blackberries bushes planted in acidic soil may be reduced.

Good Neighbors:
Almond trees, beans, blueberries, cherry trees, chives, grapes, lemon balm, mint, oak trees, pear trees, peas, strawberries.

Bad Neighbors:
Plants that can't handle acidic soil.

Known Benefits:
Blackberries create a perfect habitat for parasitic wasps, so plant them near your garden and you'll find you have less pests to deal with.

Borage

Borage is an easy to grow annual with bright blue flowers. It's generally grown as an ornamental plant, but the leaves are edible and are said to have the flavor of cucumbers. Harvest the leaves while they're young, before the prickly fuzz develops.

Even if you don't plan on eating borage, it can be beneficial to have in the garden. It attracts bees and other pollinators and is a good companion for strawberries and squash. It's also a good companion for tomatoes because it repels the tomato hornworm.

Good Neighbors:
Most plants, including cabbage, cucumbers, fruit trees, squash, strawberries, tomatoes.

Bad Neighbors:
No known bad neighbors.

Known Benefits:
Attracts pollinators and repels pests like the tomato hornworm and cabbage worms. It also attracts predatory wasps and helps protect the roots of nearby plants from disease.

Broccoli

Broccoli belongs to the Brassica oleracea family, which also encompasses Brussels sprouts, cauliflower, collard greens, kale and kohlrabi.

Avoid planting other Brassica family plants near broccoli because they'll compete for nutrients. You can sometimes get away with it in rich soil, but try this in a garden with poor soil and you'll have nothing but trouble. Other heavy feeding plants like asparagus, corn and watermelon should also be planted away from broccoli. Strawberries have also been known to slow the growth of broccoli.

There are a wide variety of plants that can be used as companion plants with broccoli. Celery, onions and potatoes are all said to improve the flavor of broccoli. Beets are a good companion plant for broccoli because they don't require much calcium, while broccoli needs a lot of it. Turnips can be used as a trap crop that draws cabbage flies away from broccoli and herbs with strong scents like basil, dill, garlic, mint, rosemary and sage repel harmful insects. Buckwheat can be planted to attract hoverflies that will eliminate pests that attack broccoli.

Rosemary is considered one of the best companions for broccoli because it helps broccoli reach its full potential. Sage is also said to enhance the growth of broccoli.

Good Neighbors:

Anise, basil, beets, buckwheat, celery, chamomile, chives, clover, dill, garlic, hyssop, lavender, lemon balm, lettuce, mint, onions, potatoes, rhubarb, rosemary, sage, spinach, turnips.

Bad Neighbors:
Other Brassica family plants, asparagus, corn, kale, lettuce, mint, Nightshade family plants, radishes, strawberries, watermelon.

Known Benefits:
When broccoli is planted near lettuce, both crops show increased yields. Broccoli plants can be used to provide midday shade to plants that have trouble in direct sunlight like lettuce and spinach.

Brussels Sprouts

Brussels sprouts are another member of the Brassica oleracea family, which isn't surprising when you consider cabbage comes from the same family and they look like mini cabbages. These plants are prolific growers and can produce upwards of 3 pounds of sprouts per plant under prime growing conditions. They're heavy feeders and require plenty of nitrogen in the soil, so it's a good idea to plant them in succession to peas or beans. Try planting beets close to Brussels sprouts to ensure they have the nutrients they need to grow.

Insects love Brussels sprouts and have been known to attack every part of the plant. To repel aphids, squash bugs and white flies, try planting nasturtium nearby. Marigolds ward off a bunch of different pests and garlic is thought to repel Japanese beetles and aphids. Rosemary, sage, dill and peppermint can also be used to repel pests. Onions can be used to keep aphids away.

Chamomile can be planted close to Brussels sprouts to improve their flavor, but you're going to have to be careful. This plant creeps stealthily along the ground and will quickly spread out, so all you're going to need is a plant or two in order to set things in motion. If you don't want the hassle of trying to keep chamomile in check, try garlic instead. It's also said to help improve the flavor of Brussels sprouts.

Don't plant Brussels sprouts near other plants in their family, pole beans, strawberries or nightshade vegetables like tomatoes, peppers and eggplant. Brassica oleracea plants compete for nutrients and may stunt each other's growth. Brussels sprouts release chemicals into the soil that may impede the growth of nightshade vegetables.

Good Neighbors:
Anise, beets, bush beans, chamomile, chives, clover, dill, garlic, hyssop, lavender, marigolds, mint, mustard, nasturtium, onions, peas, peppermint, rhubarb, rosemary, sage, thyme.

Bad Neighbors:
Other Brassica oleracea family members, corn, kale, Nightshade vegetables, pole beans, radishes, strawberries.

Known Benefits:
None.

Buckwheat

Don't let the word "wheat" in the name fool you. Buckwheat may resemble wheat when it's ground into flour, but it isn't a grain. It's actually the fruit of the buckwheat plant that's harvested and ground up. The main draw of buckwheat flour is it's gluten-free and is a good alternative for those looking to eliminate gluten from their diet.

Buckwheat thrives in poor soil where most crops would fail. It can be used as a cover crop to improve soil quality and is able to draw in beneficial insects. The ability of buckwheat to draw in hoverflies benefits broccoli, green beans and potatoes, amongst other vegetables.

Good Neighbors:
Broccoli, green beans, potatoes, pumpkins, squash, strawberries.

Bad Neighbors:
No known bad neighbors.

Known Benefits:
Draws in beneficial insects like ladybugs, hoverflies, minute pirate bugs and pollinators, while suppressing weed growth by growing quickly and smothering weeds. Buckwheat deters pests from a number of crops. Another benefit of buckwheat is its ability to take phosphorous from the soil and convert it into a more plant-friendly form.

Bush Beans

Bush beans, also known as snap beans or string beans, are bean plants that grow in squat bushes that don't have to be trellised in order to promote growth. They rank amongst the most popular vegetables grown in gardens across the United States. Bush beans reach maturity quickly, usually within 7 weeks of planting, and all of the beans mature and are harvested over a period of a couple weeks.

Planting potatoes, rosemary or marigolds near bush beans can help eliminate bush beetles. Summer savory is also known to deter bush beetles and is believed to improve the flavor of beans grown nearby. Planting cauliflower near beans will deter harmful insects and draw in beneficial ones. Chamomile will draw in hover flies that dine on aphids. Rhubarb will repel black flies.

Fennel, garlic, onions and shallots shouldn't be planted in close proximity to bush beans because they can stunt the beans growth. Avoid planting cucumbers, lettuce, tomatoes and other legumes in succession with bush beans, as they can increase the levels of a fungus known as sclerotinia in the soil.

Good Neighbors:

Anise, beets, blackberries, Brussels sprouts, cabbage, cantaloupe, carrots, cauliflower, celery, chamomile, coriander, corn, eggplant, grapes, leeks, marigolds, potatoes, pumpkins, raspberries, rhubarb, rosemary, strawberries, summer savory, tansy.

Bad Neighbors:

Chives, cucumbers, fennel, garlic, legumes, lettuce, onions, pole beans, shallots, tomatoes.

Known Benefits:

Bean plants pull nitrogen from the air and add it to the soil. This will benefit plants that need a lot of nitrogen like blackberries, corn, eggplant and grains that are planted right after beans have been grown. Green beans will repel Colorado potato beetles.

Cabbage

Cabbage is a cool-season crop that can be grown while the weather's still cool in the spring or once the weather starts to turn cold in the fall. Cabbage is another member of the Brassica oleracea family and it needs plenty of nutrients, just like the rest of them. Don't plant it near plants from the same family or other plants with heavy nutrient requirements. This is especially important in areas with soil of questionable quality.

Cabbage has a tendency to attract snails and slugs. Keep this in mind when choosing companion plants for cabbage and select plants that either repel snails and slugs or aren't susceptible to them. Garlic and lettuce has been shown to repel the diamondback moth, which attacks certain varieties of cabbage. Celery and marigolds are also known to repel moths that attack cabbage, while nasturtiums can be used as a trap crop for aphids. Onions repel insects and may even keep larger pests like rodents and rabbits at bay. Borage repels cabbage worms and tomato hornworms, while attracting predatory wasps. Hyssop is another plant that's beneficial to grow around cabbage.

Clover draws in predatory insects that protect cabbage by reducing cabbageworm and aphid population. When planting clover around cabbage, be sure to plant the cabbage first and give it time to get established before planting clover. This will help ensure your cabbage plants reach their full potential.

Mint is a good neighbor that helps cabbage plants grow and thrive. Potatoes, thyme and sage can also be planted with cabbage to aid growth.

Good Neighbors:

Anise, asparagus, beets, beans, borage, celery, chamomile, chives, clover, coriander, dill, garlic, hyssop, lavender, lettuce, marigold, mint, nasturtiums, onions, potatoes, rosemary, rhubarb, sage, tansy, thyme.

Bad Neighbors:

Other Brassica plants, corn, grapes, nightshade vegetables, plants that are susceptible to snails and slugs, radishes, strawberries.

Known Benefits:

Cabbage aids with the growth of tansy when planted nearby.

Cantaloupe

Cantaloupes is a warm-season crops that needs plenty of sunlight, moisture and heat. When given the proper amount of all three, you'll be rewarded with melons that are bursting with flavor and put the ones sold in grocery stores to shame. Cantaloupes can be trellised, but you're going to need something sturdy. Trellises for cantaloupe should be 6 to 8 feet tall and have adequate support to hold up the weight of the melons once they start to grow.

Cantaloupes are prolific growers and heavy feeders, so it's important to make sure they're well-fed and have room to grow. Beans add nitrogen to the soil, which is beneficial to cantaloupe. Corn doesn't add a whole lot to the soil, but it does attract pollinating insects and can be planted so it provide shade from the afternoon heat.

Squash bugs and squash vine borers are common pests that attack cantaloupe plants, chewing through both the vines and foliage. Striped cucumber beetles also attack the plants. Nasturtium repel squash bugs, cucumber beetles and possibly aphids, while attracting predatory insects and has the added bonus of enhancing the flavor of cantaloupe plants it's planted close to. Tansy can be used to repel cucumber beetles and squash bugs. Catnip, dill and radishes can all be used to repel squash bugs.

Don't plant potatoes too close to your cantaloupe plants, as it can inhibit growth.

Good Neighbors:
Beans, catnip, corn, dill, lemon balm, mustard, nasturtium, radishes, tansy.

Bad Neighbors:
Cucumbers, potatoes.

Known Benefits:
No known benefits.

Carrots

Carrots are a root vegetable that grow best in sandy soil that allows the roots to freely penetrate deep into the ground. Make sure the soil is free of stones, as rocks can cause deformities in carrots as they attempt to grow in a different direction. Don't add fresh manure to the soil right before planting carrots, as it can cause the carrot to split and grow legs. Turn manure into the garden plot at the end of the season and let it sit through the winter instead of adding it at the beginning.

Celery releases a chemical into the soil that slows the growth of carrots. Both celery and corn are carriers of yellow aster disease, which can stunt the growth of carrots, making their roots bitter and excessively hairy. Chives, on the other hand, will improve carrot growth and flavor while repelling both aphids and carrot flies. Carrots and radishes are good neighbors because radishes grow quickly and loosen up the soil. This paves the way for the carrots, making it easier for them to penetrate deep into the soil. Carrots and lettuce are good neighbors because their roots grow at different depths and they won't compete for nutrients. When planted near peppers, carrots are said to improve their flavor.

Planting carrots near tomatoes will help the tomatoes grow, but may slow the growth of the carrots if you plant the carrots too close. However, carrots grown near tomatoes have better flavor. Some sources list this as a benefit, while others state carrots and tomatoes are bad neighbors.

Aromatic plants like leeks, onions and sage repel flying insects like the carrot fly. Parsnips, on the other hand will draw carrot flies in, so avoid planting them in close proximity to carrots. Dill should also be avoided, because carrots and dill are both from the Umbelliferae family and can cross-pollinate one another.

Rosemary is said to repel carrot flies, but may cause problems when planted near carrots. Rosemary leaves can be trimmed and spread around carrot plants to keep the flies away without inhibiting the growth of the carrots. Some sources say rosemary actually helps carrots grow stronger when planted close to them, so you might want to try it in a small area to see what happens.

Good Neighbors:

Beans, chives, cucumbers, garlic, leeks, lettuce, marigolds, onions, peas, peppers, radishes, sage, tomatoes.

Bad Neighbors:

Anise, aster, celery, corn, dill, parsnips, potatoes, rosemary, watermelons.

Known Benefits:

Carrots can attract beneficial insects to the garden, but this only happens when carrots are flowering. They repel both the leek moth and the onion fly.

Catnip

Catnip is well-known because of its propensity to attract cats, but it can also be planted as a companion plant in order to attract beneficial insects and drive away undesirable ones. It drives away aphids, so it's a good choice to plant near squash, tomatoes and other plants susceptible to aphid attack.

Rats and mice don't like catnip, so it can be planted around fruit trees and other crops that may be attacked by rodents. Just be careful where you plant it. If you have a lot of cats in your neighborhood, you might attract them into your garden. You can use this to your benefit by planting catnip away from your garden to lure cats out.

Good Neighbors:
Beets, cantaloupe, eggplant, fruit trees, lettuce, squash, strawberries, tomatoes.

Bad Neighbors:
No known bad neighbors.

Known Benefits:
Attracts an insect known as the lacewing that eats aphids and mites. It also attracts bees and butterflies. Catnip deters aphids, Colorado potato beetles, flea beetles, Japanese beetles, squash bugs and weevils. Mice and rats also avoid catnip.

Cauliflower

Cauliflower is a cool weather crop that's frost tolerant. It looks similar to broccoli, which should come as no surprise since it's from the Brassica family like broccoli. Unlike broccoli, cauliflower only develops one head per plant. Avoid planting cauliflower and broccoli close to one another because since they're from the same family they're vulnerable to the same diseases and pests. It's like painting a giant target on your cauliflower and broccoli crops and inviting every insect around to come calling. Another reason to keep them apart is both plants are heavy feeders and will compete for nutrients in the soil.

Cauliflower crops need to be blanched as the head begins to form. This is done by wrapping the leaves around the cauliflower head and tying them in place. Blanching cauliflower heads ensures the heads are soft and white when they're harvested. Failure to blanch cauliflower will result in heads that are bitter and tough.

Plant celery, dill or sage near cauliflower to keep cabbage worms at bay. You'll know cabbage worms have made their way into your cauliflower crop when you see white butterflies with several black markings on their wings flitting about. Celery can be a bit difficult to grow, but is a great cool-weather companion for cauliflower. Hyssop is another good neighbor that will keep pest insects away.

Avoid planting garlic or rue because their roots release a chemical that stunts the growth of cauliflower plants. Peas are similarly able to stunt cauliflower's growth. Tomatoes require a lot of nutrients and can also stunt cauliflower plant growth. Strawberries attract slugs that will prey on your cauliflower.

Good Neighbors:
Anise, beets, bush beans, celery, chamomile, chives, clover, dill, hyssop, lavender, lemon balm, lettuce, mint, onions, rhubarb, sage, spinach, turnips.

Bad Neighbors:
Brassica family plants, eggplant, garlic, kale, Nightshade plants, peas, radishes, rue, strawberries, tomatoes.

Known Benefits:
Planting cauliflower and beans together deters harmful insects that attack both plants and will bring in more helpful insects. Some people like plant their cauliflower between two rows of beans.

Celery

Celery is a long-season crop that can be a bit sensitive to changes in its environment. Celery prefers cool temperatures and constant moisture and may turn woody or go to seed if its needs aren't met. Blanch your celery stalks by tying the leaves around them or otherwise covering them for a couple weeks before harvest. Celery that isn't blanched will be strongly bitter.

Insects are a big threat to celery crops, as there are a variety of pests that love to prey on their tasty leaves and roots. Marigolds and nasturtiums will drive away a number of pests, while drawing in predatory wasps and other beneficial insects. Onions are also beneficial in this regard.

Carrots suffer when planted close to celery because celery releases chemicals into the soil that slows the growth of carrots. Celery can catch a disease known as yellow aster disease from asters and carrots, so be sure to keep them spread apart. On the opposite end of the spectrum, green beans and peas assist celery plants by adding nitrogen to the soil.

Good Neighbors:
Broccoli, bush beans, cauliflower, cucumbers, kale, kohlrabi, leeks, marigolds, nasturtiums, onions, peas, turnips.

Bad Neighbors:
Asters, carrots, corn.

Known Benefits:

Celery is able to draw in beneficial insects, making it a desirable neighbor for a variety of plants. When celery is planted near broccoli, the flavor of the broccoli may improve. Celery is also able to repel cabbage worms.

Chamomile

There are two basic types of chamomile: German chamomile and Roman chamomile. German chamomile is an annual bushy shrub that can grow up to 4' in height, while Roman chamomile is grown perennially and only reaches a foot in height. The flowers of the chamomile plant look like small white daisies and they have the characteristic scent of chamomile, which is sweet and reminiscent of apples.

The dried flowers of the chamomile plant can be made into tea, but be forewarned. Those who are allergic to ragweed may want to steer clear of chamomile because the pollen of the chamomile plant can have a similar effect.

Chamomile is said to increase essential oil production in a number of plants, which improves their smell and flavor. Brussels sprouts are good neighbors with chamomile because the flavor of the sprouts improves when chamomile is planted nearby. Cucumbers are also a good choice as a neighbor because chamomile repels the cucumber beetle. Mint is another plant that thrives when planted in close proximity to chamomile.

Tomatoes, beans and roses often suffer under the burden of aphid attacks. Chamomile can be planted nearby to attract hover flies that dine on aphids.

Good Neighbors:
Beans, Brassica family plants, cucumbers, lavender, mint, onions, peppers, strawberries, tomatoes, roses.

Bad Neighbors:
No known bad neighbors.

Known Benefits:

Chamomile is said to improve essential oil production in nearby plants, which improves their scent and flavor. It also repels cucumber beetles and attracts hover flies that eat aphids.

Chives

Chives are an herb that looks and tastes similar to a green onion when chopped up and added to culinary dishes. Both the scapes and the unopened flower buds can be consumed. This tasty little plant is small in stature, rarely making it to more than a foot or two in height.

Chives improve the growth of carrots and tomatoes and are thought to give them a flavor a boost as well. Brassica family plants, eggplant, grapes, mustard, peppers, potatoes, rhubarb and squash also benefit from having chives nearby. They deter black spot when planted near the base of roses and drive away insects known to damage carrots and cucumbers. The insect repellent ability of chives is beneficial to blackberries, as is the ability to draw in pollinators.

Chives are known to help a variety of fruit trees. Apple trees in particular benefit from chives because they help prevent apple scab.

Good Neighbors:
Almonds, apples, Brassica family plants, blackberries, carrots, cucumbers, eggplant, fruit trees, grapes, lettuce, mustard, parsley, peppers, potatoes, rhubarb, roses, spinach, squash, tomatoes.

Bad Neighbors:
Asparagus, beans, peas.

Known Benefits:
Known to repel a variety of insects, including aphids, carrot flies, Colorado potato beetles, Japanese beetles and

cucumber beetles. Attracts bees. When planted near fruit trees, they help prevent apple scab and drive away boring insects.

Clover

If you have a lawn, you're probably familiar with clover. The clover plant grows quickly and spreads rapidly, making it a good cover crop, but you've got to be careful not to let it get out of control. Those who have battled clover growing in their lawn known this all too well. One day there are a handful of little clover plants and seemingly overnight, they've spread out to become large patches.

If you're lucky, you may find a 4-leaf clover, but it's going to take some work. Only 1 in 10,000 clover leaves have four leaves instead of three.

Clover works well when planted in and around most vegetables and trees. Grapes do well when clover is planted beneath them. Clover's propensity to draw in predatory insects protects cabbage by reducing cabbageworm and aphid population.

Good Neighbors:
Broccoli, cabbage, cauliflower, grapes, leeks, pumpkins.

Bad Neighbors:
Your lawn.

Known Benefits:
Draws in predatory ground beetles and other beneficial insects, while driving away aphids. Clover is technically a legume and can convert nitrogen into a form plants can absorb.

Coriander (Cilantro)

Coriander is an annual herb that can grow to a couple feet in height. The leaves of the plant are known as **cilantro** and the seeds are called **coriander**. All parts of the coriander plant are edible, including the leaves, stems and seeds. Most people find the aroma and taste of the leaves to be pleasant, but there are some who find it extremely unappealing.

Planting legumes or anise near coriander can help aid the growth of the coriander plant. Planting coriander near asparagus and spinach can help those plants grow. Avoid planting dill near coriander because there's a chance of cross-pollination. Fennel may stunt the growth of coriander.

Good Neighbors:
Anise, asparagus, beans, cabbage, lettuce, peas, spinach, tomatoes.

Bad Neighbors:
Dill, fennel.

Known Benefits:
Coriander deters asparagus beetles, aphids, Colorado potato beetles and some of the other beetles that attack plants, while attracting beneficial insects like ladybugs, parasitic wasps and hoverflies. The insect attracting and repelling properties alone are a good reason to keep coriander in a garden.

Corn

Corn is fairly easy to grow, but you're going to need plenty of garden space to plant these voracious feeders. Leave at least a foot of space between plants. You'll only get 2 to 3 ears of corn per plant, so allocate garden space accordingly. Since corn grows tall, it can be used to provide shade to plants that prefer protection from the midday and afternoon sun. Spinach and lettuce benefit from being grown in the shade of corn.

Corn makes a good companion for pole beans, as it can be grown to provide a natural trellis for the beans to climb as they grow. Pumpkins can also be planted at the same time as the beans to help corn retain moisture in its roots and crowd out weeds. This technique is known as the "Three Sisters Garden."

Vining plants like cantaloupe, cucumbers, squash and melons can be planted around the outside of a corn patch and then trained to grow through the outer rows of corn. It'll make walking through the corn a bit difficult, but it does maximize space. Alfalfa is a good neighbor because it sends roots deep beyond the roots of the corn and fixes nitrogen and other nutrients into the soil while providing shade and pest protection.

Planting tomatoes and corn close together may attract more tomato fruit worms and corn ear worms when planted together. The two worms are similar and it becomes more likely they'll show up when tomatoes and corn are within close proximity. Plant geraniums near corn to keep cabbage worms off your corn. Avoid planting corn around smaller plants that need full sunlight because the corn will block them from getting the light they need once it matures.

Good Neighbors:

Alfalfa, bush beans, cantaloupe, cucumbers, dill, geraniums, legumes, lettuce, marigolds, melons, mustard, parsley, peas, pole beans, pumpkins, soybeans, spinach, squash, sunflowers, tansy, watermelons.

Bad Neighbors:

Asters, beets, Brassica family plants, carrots, celery, tomatoes.

Known Benefits:

Corn produces a lot of pollen, so it attracts pollinating insects. It grows to tall heights and can be planted close together, so it can be used to provide shade from the midday heat.

Cranberries

When most people think of growing cranberries, they think of cranberry bogs with the bright red berries floating on the surface of the water. What many people don't realize is this is a method used to make harvesting the berries easier and has little to do with the growth phase of cranberries.

As long as you're willing to do a little soil preparation to ensure your cranberries will have low pH and high levels of organic material, cranberries may be able to grown in your garden. Cranberries prefer sandy soil and have an extremely shallow root system that can tolerate flooding, but prefers lightly moist soil during the growing season. Cranberries prefer acidic soil with a pH between 4.5 and 5.0 and can be grown alongside blueberries, raspberries, rhubarb and strawberries.

Good Neighbors:
Blueberries, raspberries, rhubarb, strawberries.

Bad Neighbors:
Plants that can't handle acidic soil.

Known Benefits:
No known benefits.

Cucumbers

Cucumbers rank amongst the easiest garden vegetables to grow and they'll grow prolifically given enough sunlight and water. Cucumbers feed heavily and require soil that's kept consistently moist. Vining varieties of cucumbers can be trellised to provide room for companion plants.

Sage and potatoes both can stunt the growth of cucumbers. Sage and other aromatic herbs can have a negative impact on the flavor of cucumbers grown close-by. Dill is an exception to this rule and is believed to improve the flavor of cucumbers. Squash and melons are susceptible to similar pest attacks and diseases as cucumbers, so avoid planting them nearby. It's a good idea to rotate your garden space to ensure you don't plant cucumbers, squash or melons in an area within a three year period. It's also a bad idea to plant watermelon close to cucumbers because both plants are susceptible to cucumber beetles and you don't want to create a large beacon for these beetles in your garden.

Peas are a good crop to plant before you plant cucumbers. Let the peas grow until they start to lose steam and production slows. Snip the pea plants off at the base and plant the cucumbers close enough to where they can benefit from the nitrogen released by the peas.

Cucumbers can be grown around corn to help ward off at least some insects. The corn will shade the cucumbers from the midday heat. Chives repel cucumber beetles. Nasturtiums can also be planted to repel insects and as a trap crop for aphids.

Hot peppers are a good companion plant for cucumbers because they ward off root rot and other diseases.

Good Neighbors:
Beets, borage, carrots, celery, chamomile, chives, corn, dill, hot peppers, kohlrabi, marigolds, nasturtiums, onions, peas, radishes, sunflowers, tansy.

Bad Neighbors:
Beans, melons, potatoes, sage, squash, watermelon.

Known Benefits:
Cucumbers repel pest insects and may repel larger pests like rodents.

Dill

Dill is an aromatic herb from the parsley family that can be grown as either an annual or a perennial. The leaves and seeds of the dill plant can be used fresh or they can be dried and used to add flavor to food. Dill requires warm climates and well-drained fertile soil to thrive.

Dill may help the growth of asparagus, Brassica family members, corn, cucumbers, lettuce and onions. Carrots and fennel are from the Umbelliferae family and can cross-pollinate with dill, which can have unpredictable results. Dill can also cross-pollinate with cilantro, which can ruin both crops.

You may have already noticed tomatoes are listed in both the good neighbors and bad neighbors lists below. Young dill plants can enhance the growth of tomatoes, but don't leave them in the ground too long. Once dill matures, it can begin to compete with tomatoes for nutrients and will eventually end up stunting the growth of the tomatoes. Mature dill also attracts tomato hornworms, which is another reason to keep it away from your tomatoes.

Good Neighbors:

Asparagus, Brassica family members, cantaloupe, corn, cucumbers, lettuce, mustard, onions, tomatoes, turnips.

Bad Neighbors:

Carrots, coriander, eggplant, fennel, peppers, potatoes, tomatoes.

Known Benefits:

Dill repels aphids, cabbage worms, root maggots and squash bugs and can bring a number of beneficial insects into a garden, including ladybugs, pollinators and parasitic wasps. It improves the flavor of cucumbers when planted as a companion.

Eggplant

Eggplant is a nightshade vegetable that grows best in a sunny environment with well-drained soil. Eggplant can get very heavy when loaded with fruit, so it's a good idea to stake your plants while they're young. It's important to make sure you harvest eggplant at the right time during its growth cycle because too early or too late of a harvest will result in a bitter tasting fruit.

Beans fix nitrogen into the soil, which will help fill the heavy nutritional needs of eggplant. It's best to plant beans first and then turn them into the soil before planting eggplant in succession. Green beans have the added benefit of driving the Colorado potato beetle away. Try planting bush beans near the base of the eggplant, so the beans fill in the space between the ground and the taller eggplants. Spinach can be planted for the same purpose. Thyme is also said to help eggplant thrive.

Catnip is a good neighbor to eggplant because it drives away flea beetles and other insects that may attack eggplant. Marigolds drive away pests and attract a number of beneficial insects.

Brassica oleracea vegetables contain chemicals that can inhibit the growth of eggplant. Eggplant shouldn't be planted near apricots because it can pass diseases to the apricot trees. Tomatoes, peppers and potatoes attract pests that attack eggplants and should be avoided.

Good Neighbors:

Beans, catnip, chives, garlic, green beans, marigolds, radishes, spinach, thyme.

Bad Neighbors:

Apricots, Brassica oleracea plants, dill, peppers, potatoes, raspberries, thyme, tomatoes.

Known Benefits:

No known benefits.

Fennel

Drive far enough down a highway in the United States, Canada or Europe and there's a pretty good chance you'll come across a fennel plant. Fennel is a perennial herb with yellow flowers and wispy, feathery leaves that tastes similar to anise, but isn't quite as strong. Both the bulbs of the plant and the seeds can be eaten.

Fennel isn't a good companion to most fruits and vegetables. You have to be careful even if you grow it in a container because the seeds will be dispersed far and wide if it's allowed to go to seed. There are people who report growing fennel alongside herbs like cilantro, dill, mustard and oregano, but your mileage may vary.

Good Neighbors:
None.

Bad Neighbors:
Most plants. Beans, coriander, kohlrabi and tomatoes are particularly susceptible.

Known Benefits:
Fennel attracts ladybugs, damsel bugs, parasitic wasps and butterflies and repels aphids. It can also be planted near a dog house or kennel to repel fleas.

Garlic

Garlic is relatively easy to grow in the home garden and is able to be grown in a variety of soil conditions. Instead of growing it from seeds, most gardeners choose to plant cloves, which are the individual pieces you find when you break apart a head of garlic. Each clove produces one bulb. Garlic is normally planted in the fall and harvested the next season.

Almond, apricot and apple trees benefit from garlic's ability to ward off insects, as do a wide variety of other vegetables. Garlic has been known to stunt the growth of peas, so provide plenty of space between them. Potatoes benefit from having garlic nearby because it helps prevent potato blight.

Good Neighbors:
Almonds, apples, apricots, beets, broccoli, Brussels sprouts, cabbage, carrots, eggplant, kale, kohlrabi, fruit trees, parsnips, peppers, potatoes, raspberries, roses, tomatoes.

Bad Neighbors:
Asparagus, beans, cauliflower, grapes, peas.

Known Benefits:
Garlic wards off a number of insects, including aphids, Colorado potato beetles, the diamondback moth, Japanese beetles and the Mexican bean beetle and is able to deter some larger pests like moles and even rabbits. It contains sulfur, a natural fungicide that protects the roots of plants nearby from disease.

Geraniums

Geraniums are perennial flowers that are easy to grow and can be used as ground cover in a garden. They feature brightly colored flowers and are equally at home in ornamental gardens and functional gardens alike. There are geraniums available that'll grow under most conditions.

Deadheading, which is the trimming of flowers as they start to die, will help promote future flower growth and keep flowers blooming for a longer period of time. Removing dying flower heads allows geranium flowers to dedicate more resources to growing new ones.

Corn, grapes and roses all benefit from the ability of geraniums to lure pests away from nearby plants. You may be able to use geraniums to help other plants that are under siege as well. Be aware that geraniums can be toxic to both cats and dogs. The oils found in the plants can cause skin and eye irritation and may poison animals that consume them. Peppers benefit from the pest repellent properties of geraniums and the ability of the flowers to bring pollinators into the garden.

Good Neighbors:
Corn, grapes, peppers, roses.

Bad Neighbors:
No known problems, but be aware geraniums can be toxic to pets. If you've got dogs or cats that roam freely, you may want to explore other options.

Known Benefits:

Geraniums attract beetles like the Japanese beetles and cabbage worms and can be used as a trap plant to lure them away from other plants. White geraniums seem to work best for Japanese beetles. The brightly-colored flowers of geraniums lure in pollinators.

Grapes

Once you pluck a ripe grape off a vine you've grown and pop it into your mouth, you'll instantly be hooked on growing grapes. As long as you've got a sunny plot of land and healthy soil, there's a good chance you can grow grapes. When choosing the variety you want to grow, make sure you pick one suited to your climate zone. Choosing the right variety could be the difference between having plentiful harvests and struggling to get your grapevines established.

Grapes should be trellised or grown on an overhead arbor. With all that empty space beneath your grapevines, it would be a shame to let it go to waste. Luckily, there are a number of plants that can be grown around grapes that will be of benefit. Tour a vineyard during the early spring and you may see the yellow flowers of mustard plants growing amongst the grapes. Mustard is often planted as a companion to grapes because it's a great cover crop and can be turned into the soil to provide nutrients to the grapes.

Beans and peas add nitrogen to the soil, which will aid grapes in growth. Clover improves the soil and can be beneficial to grapes. Plant soil-enhancing plants in moderation for best results.

Chives are good neighbors because they aid with the growth of grapes and drive away aphids. Geraniums, basil and oregano are also a good choice thanks to their ability to drive away pests like Japanese beetles and worms that will make short work of grapes.

Cabbage, lettuce and garlic can all stunt the growth of grapes, so leave plenty of space between them. Mint should be kept clear of grapes because grapes will sometimes take up some of the flavor of mint.

Good Neighbors:
Basil, beans, blackberries, chives, clover, geraniums, hyssop, mustard, oregano, peas.

Bad Neighbors:
Cabbage, garlic, lettuce, mint, radishes.

Known Benefits:
No known benefits.

Hyssop

Hyssop is a perennial shrub with bright blue, pink, purple or white flowers. Hyssop prefers loose, dry soil and lots of sunlight. It adds a touch of color to your garden and can add a lot of flavor to soups, stews and other culinary dishes it's added to. Make sure you know what you're planting, as there are some plants that are grown in the United States that are called hyssop that are inedible.

Because it draws in pollinators and repels pest insects, hyssop is beneficial to a number of plants. It helps grapes grow and keeps pests off of plants it's planted close to. Planting Brassica family plants near hyssop will improve the growth rate of the hyssop.

Good Neighbors:
Brassica family plants, grapes.

Bad Neighbors:
Radishes.

Known Benefits:
Deters pests and draws in bees, hummingbirds and other pollinating insects.

Kale

Kale isn't just good for you; the large, frilly leaves of the kale plant look amazing growing in your garden. There's little that's more satisfying than seeing these big, beautiful greens sprout up and develop into mature plants.

If you're looking for a cold-hardy plant that can be grown in the early spring and late fall in most regions, kale's the ticket. It prefers full sun, but can tolerate shade and actually tastes better if it's seen a frost or two. If you live in warmer climates, kale can be grown there, but may not grow as large as it does in cooler areas.

Avoid planting kale near Brassica family plants because they share a lot of pests and diseases with kale. Instead, plant kale around beets, celery, garlic, onions and potatoes. Onions and garlic repel a number of insects that attack kale and may even prevent rabbits from sneaking up and nibbling on their leaves.

Good Neighbors:
Beets, celery, garlic, onions, potatoes.

Bad Neighbors:
Brassica family plants, peppers, radishes, strawberries.

Known Benefits:
No known benefits.

Kohlrabi

I can't help but wonder who was the first person to try kohlrabi. At a glance, the bulbous stem of the kohlrabi plant looks anything but edible. Whoever it was must have been pleasantly surprised when they bit into it to find it tastes like a sweeter version of a turnip. The leaves are also edible and can be cooked or steamed in a manner similar to how you'd prepare kale.

Kohlrabi is a cool-weather crop that grows rapidly when conditions are optimal. Plant kohlrabi in the early spring or late fall and you'll have bulbs that are ready to eat within 6 weeks. This hardy vegetable prefers full sun and well-drained soil.

Kohlrabi is good neighbors with beets because they take nutrients from the soil in a different manner from one another and won't compete over the same nutrients. Kohlrabi sets shallow roots that gather water and nutrients near the surface, while beets dig down deeper and get their nutrients below the reach of kohlrabi.

Plant garlic and onions near kohlrabi to keep many of the insects that attack kohlrabi at bay. Kohlrabi is a member of the Brassica oleracea family, so avoid planting it near other Brassicas, as they'll act like a beacon to pests.

Good Neighbors:
Anise, beets, celery, chamomile, chives, cucumbers, dill, garlic, hyssop, lavender, mint, onions, rhubarb.

Bad Neighbors:
Brassica family plants, corn, kale, eggplants, fennel, Nightshade plants, radishes, pole beans.

Known Benefits:
No known benefits.

Lavender

Lavender will add a touch of purple to your home garden and can be grown as either a decorative or functional plant. It's drought-resistant and is a good choice for dry, arid areas like much of Southern California. Lavender is grown as a perennial in the Western states, but doesn't usually make it through the winter in cooler locations. When growing lavender, make sure it has full sun and well-drained soil.

Use lavender to control pest populations in your garden by planting it to draw in beneficial insects and repel pests. Lavender grows fairly tall, so it can be planted to provide shade for cool-season crops like Brassica family plants. Roses are good companions because they won't compete with lavender for nutrients.

Mint and other spreading plants may be problematic around lavender because they'll eventually start competing with lavender for nutrients. If you want to grow mint in close proximity to lavender, try growing the mint in a raised container.

Good Neighbors:
Brassica family members, chamomile, onions, roses, squash, tomatoes, yarrow.

Bad Neighbors:
Mint.

Known Benefits:

Wards off slugs, moths and caterpillars. Attracts parasitic wasps, pollinators and hoverflies. Deer don't like lavender and may steer clear of a garden to avoid it.

Leeks

Leeks are close cousins to the onion, but feature a toned down, mild flavor that many people find preferable to the bite of onions. The stem is the edible portion of the leek. The stems should be blanched to prevent them from turning bitter. As leeks grow, push soil up around the stems to make sure they stay covered.

Carrots and leeks mutually benefit one another. We already discussed the ability of leeks to repel the carrot fly. Carrots are beneficial to leeks because they mask the smell of leeks and prevent leek moths and onion flies from honing in on them.

Leeks may stunt the growth of peas when planted too close.

Good Neighbors:
Apples, bush beans, carrots, celery, clover, onions, strawberries, tomatoes.

Bad Neighbors:
Peas, pole beans.

Known Benefits:
Repels carrot flies.

Lemon Balm

Lemon balm is a member of the mint family, which means you need to keep it under control or it can really take off. It isn't as invasive as most mint family plants, but can get unruly if left to its own accord. It's important to keep younger lemon balm plants trimmed back, as they can grow to heights approaching 5' as they mature. Lemon balm is grown as a perennial in warmer climates, but can be grown as an annual in areas where temperatures dip below freezing.

Taller plants that provide shade are good neighbors to lemon balm because it prefers to be out of the hot afternoon sun. This is especially important in areas where summer heat approaches 100° F.

Lemon balm is said to improve both the growth rate and the flavor of tomatoes when planted nearby. It's compatible with most plants, but is especially beneficial to the plants listed in the good neighbors list. Most gardens could benefit from having a lemon balm plant or two nearby. If you don't want to deal with the hassle of keeping it trimmed back all the time, try growing it in a container.

Good Neighbors:
Blackberries, broccoli, cauliflower, melons, squash, taller plants that can provide shade, tomatoes.

Bad Neighbors:
Watermelons.

Known Benefits:

Repels pests and calls in pollinators, parasitic wasps and ladybugs.

Lettuce

Lettuce is one of the easiest plants to grow in most gardens, so it should be no surprise it ranks amongst the top vegetables grown in gardens. Lettuce prefers full sun and fertile, well-drained soil, but is one of a select few vegetables that can be grown in partial shade. Since lettuce is a cool weather crop, it does better when shaded from the hot afternoon sun.

Aphids are the pest most likely to attack lettuce. Herbs that repel aphids like catnip, chives, coriander and dill can all be planted near lettuce to deter aphids.

Leaf lettuce can be planted close to tomatoes to keep the soil cooler. In turn, the tomatoes will provide some much-needed shade to the lettuce when temperatures start to climb. Corn, pole beans and sunflowers can also be used to provide shade to lettuce.

Onions are another good companion plant for lettuce. You can harvest onions and plant tomatoes in the holes created by the onions or the two plants can be grown at the same time and the onions will provide protection from pests. Carrots are good companions because their roots grow at different depths than lettuce and the two plants won't compete for nutrients.

Good Neighbors:
Beets, broccoli, cabbage, carrots, catnip, cauliflower, chives, coriander, corn, dill, marigolds, onions, pole beans, radishes, strawberries, sunflowers, tomatoes.

Bad Neighbors:
Bush beans, grapes, parsley.

Known Benefits:
When broccoli is planted near lettuce, both crops show increased yields. Lettuce repels some insects, including the diamondback moth.

Marigolds

While marigolds may seem like a strange addition to an organic vegetable garden, they do have their uses. Many people don't realize this, but the blooms are actually edible and can be used in salads. Additionally, marigolds have a handful of benefits they can bestow on surrounding plants. Plus you get pretty flowers, which is an added bonus.

Marigolds emit a chemical that's a natural pesticide into the soil that repels a number of insects. They can be companion planted with lettuce, peppers, tomatoes and a variety of other plants to repel pests. The effect of marigolds lasts long after they've been removed from the soil, with some reports stating they remain in effect years after the plants have been removed. Marigolds hit aphids with a double whammy. The scent of marigolds repels aphids from landing nearby. Any aphids that do land will quickly fall prey to the hoverflies that are attracted to the flowers of the marigold plant. This benefits most plants that are susceptible to aphid attack, with roses being the plant that benefits most.

Don't turn marigolds into the soil right before you plant other plants nearby, as they may prevent other plants from growing. This effect is short-lived, so you should be able to turn marigolds into the soil at the end of harvest season and then grow plants in the same location when spring rolls around.

Good Neighbors:

Asparagus, Brussels sprouts, bush beans, cabbage, carrots, celery, corn, cucumbers, eggplant, lettuce, onions, peppers, pole beans, potatoes, pumpkins, roses, squash, tomatoes, watermelons.

Bad Neighbors:
No known bad neighbors.

Known Benefits:
The brightly colored petals of the marigold flower repel a variety of insects, while the scent of the leaves and a substance released by the roots repels pests. Marigolds deter the Japanese beetle that attacks corn, Colorado potato beetles and Mexican bean beetles and draw in ladybugs and damsel bugs that feed on aphids and parasitic wasps.

Mint

Mint is a fragrant, easy-to-grow herb. In fact, it's almost too easy to grow, as mint plants send runners everywhere and will quickly take over a garden. When growing mint in a garden to reap the benefits of companion planting, your best bet is to grow it in a container and plant the container into the soil. This will keep the roots contained, preventing the plant from sending runners out everywhere. For best results when growing mint, provide dappled shade and protection from the midday sun.

Mint gets a flavor boost from chamomile when the two are paired together. The natural flavors of tomatoes and Brassica family plants is said to improve when grown near mint.

There's no mistaking the flavor of mint, thanks in large part to the bite provided by a chemical known as **menthol** that's found in large amounts in mint plants. While most humans appreciate the flavor of menthol, it isn't so popular in the animal kingdom and drives away insects and larger pests alike. Plant mint around the border of your garden and you've just made it a lot harder for pests to find their way to the plants they want to eat. A number of plants benefit from the insect-repellent properties of mint. Roses, blackberries and tomatoes all fall into this category.

Avoid planting grapes close to mint, especially if you're growing wine grapes. The grapes may take up some of the flavor of the mint, imparting a minty aftertaste to anything made with the grapes.

Good Neighbors:

Beets, blackberries, Brassica family plants, chamomile, mustard, nettles, onions, roses, tomatoes.

Bad Neighbors:
Grapes, lavender, parsley.

Known Benefits:
Repels pest insects and attracts pollinators and damsel bugs. Spearmint and peppermint are known to repel aphids, flea beetles and cabbage moths. Mint is also said to repel mice and other rodents.

Mustard

Mustard can be grown in most soils, but does best in well-drained soil rich in organic material. Mustard plants prefer shade from the afternoon sun, so plant taller plants like corn, grapes and pole beans nearby. The shoots, stems, leaves, flowers and seeds of the mustard plant are all edible and can be added to culinary dishes as a delectable flavoring.

Having chives around will aid the growth of mustard. Mustard can be used as a cover crop that can be turned into the soil to provide nutrients to grapes and other crops with heavy nutrient requirements.

Mint will repel insects that dine on mustard greens. Mustard attracts a lot of insects and can be planted on the outer edges of a garden as a trap plant that lures insects away from your more desirable crops. If you're growing mustard because you want to consume it, aromatic herbs like dill, tansy and yarrow can be planted nearby to draw in predatory insects that will help protect the mustard plants and drive away pests.

Mustard emits a chemical that can slow the growth of certain plants. Avoid planting mustard around beets for this reason. Sunflowers and soybeans are bad neighbors to mustard because they can pass diseases like downy mildew and white rust amongst each other.

Good Neighbors:

Brussels sprouts, cantaloupe, chives, corn, dill, grapes, mint, peas, pole beans, tansy, yarrow.

Bad Neighbors:

Beets, sunflowers, soybeans.

Known Benefits:

Mustard can be used as a trap plant for a wide range of insects, including cabbage loopers and cabbageworms.

Nasturtiums

Most gardeners plant nasturtiums for their pretty red, orange and yellow flowers without ever realizing the flowers and leaves are edible. The leaves of the nasturtium plant are peppery and are best mixed with sweeter greens. The flowers are less intense and can be broken up into salads and other culinary dishes. These hardy plants are easy to grow and actually prefer poor quality soil.

Nasturtiums repel insects that attack corn, cucumbers, potatoes and a number of other plants, so they're often used as companion plants. There's contradictory information from various trusted sources regarding nasturtiums and aphids. Some sources report they drive aphids away, while others report they lure aphids in and can be used as a trap crop. In my experience, nasturtiums call in aphids like crazy and make a great trap crop.

Good Neighbors:
Apples, Brussels sprouts, cabbage, cantaloupe, carrots, celery, corn, cucumbers, potatoes, radishes, squash, watermelon.

Bad Neighbors:
No known bad neighbors.

Known Benefits:
Nasturtiums repel pest insects, including codling moths, Colorado potato beetles and cucumber beetles. They're also capable of attracting predatory wasps that can help clear the garden of pests. Nasturtiums attract aphids and can be used as a trap crop.

Onions

There are a vast number of varieties of plant that fall under the moniker "onion." Depending on the type of onion, you may find yourself eating the bulbs, globes, stalks or stems of the onion plant. There are varieties available that can be grown in most climates, so make sure the type of onion you choose is suited to the area you plan on growing it in.

Gardeners tend to get stuck on the idea that produce has to be planted in orderly rows. This is problematic because all it takes is for pests to find a single plant and the rest are history. Interspersing plants like onions between your crops can help you keep pests at bay because a large number of pests don't like onions.

A wide variety of plants benefit from the ability of onions to drive off pests, both large and small. Plant onions around the outside of garden beds to drive off pests and disperse them amongst your crops to further confuse pests that thought they'd found an easy meal. While onions are great at driving off most pests, there are a few pests like the onion fly that actually prefer onions. Keeping mint nearby should deter onion flies, but be careful not to let the mint grow out of control.

Onions have a shallow root system and can be planted in close proximity to plants that dig deeper into the soil to ensure they aren't competing for food with their neighbors. Beets and carrots are both good companions with onions for this reason. Peppers are also good companions and having onions nearby is thought to improve the flavor of the peppers.

Peas and beans are bad neighbors with onions because plants from the Allium family can stunt their growth. Be sure to leave plenty of space between these bad neighbors.

Good Neighbors:
Apples, beets, Brassica family plants, carrots, celery, chamomile, cucumbers, dill, kale, lavender, leeks, lettuce, marigolds, mint, peppers, roses, strawberries, tomatoes.

Bad Neighbors:
Asparagus, bush beans, parsley, parsnips, peas, pole beans, sage.

Known Benefits:
Onions repel a variety of insects, including aphids, Japanese beetles, root maggots and carrot flies and may even prevent larger pests like rodents and rabbits from attacking your crops.

Oregano

Oregano is an aromatic herb that grows quickly and can be used as ground cover. It requires full sun, but enjoys a bit of afternoon shade on hot days in the middle of the summer. Oregano is grown as either a perennial or an annual plant depending on how cold it gets over the winter in the area it's grown. Avoid overwatering oregano, which can lead to root rot that can kill the plant.

Pest insects find the scent of oregano repulsive, so plant it close to plants you want to afford general protection from pests. Because of its ability to quickly spread, it's best to plant oregano in a pot and then bury the pot in the ground to contain its roots.

Good Neighbors:
Most plants.

Bad Neighbors:
No known bad neighbors.

Known Benefits:
The scent of oregano drives away moths and a number of other pests. Oregano can be used to call in butterflies, hoverflies and parasitic wasps.

Parsley

Parsley is a biennial herb that provides plenty of beautiful, lush foliage when allowed to grow. Curled parsley has striking ruffled edges, while flat-leaf parsley isn't quite as impressive, but still looks good. Regardless of the type, parsley can be grown in either full sun or partial shade and prefers moist soil with plenty of organic material.

The parsleyworm caterpillar may make its way into your garden when you plant parsley. This vividly-colored black, green and yellow caterpillar will dine on parsley plants, but should be left alone because it will eventually turn into a black swallowtail butterfly that will benefit your garden as a pollinator.

Chives aid the growth of parsley plants. Planting parsley beneath your roses will enhance the scent of the roses and will deter the rose beetle.

Mint and lettuce are widely considered bad neighbors to parsley, but there are conflicting reports as to whether they can be grown together. Some people claim to grow them together with little to no problems, while others haven't been so successful.

Good Neighbors:
Apples, asparagus, chives, corn, roses, tomatoes.

Bad Neighbors:
Mint, lettuce, onions.

Known Benefits:

Draws in parasitic wasps and attracts butterflies. If allowed to flower, parsley will call in hoverflies. Parsley can be used as a trap crop for pests that normally prey on tomatoes.

Parsnips

The white, tapered root of the parsnip resembles a carrot, but has a nutty, sweet flavor. They can be used in soups, stews and salads and can be eaten raw or cooked, but are generally added to dishes that are cooked. Parsnips can be a bit finicky to grow and require loose soil that's rich in organic material. Leave parsnips in the ground to overwinter and you'll be rewarded with sweet and flavorful vegetables that arguably the best the carrot family has to offer.

Root maggots are one of the biggest enemies of parsnips. These maggots can't be deterred through companion planting. You may be able to sprinkle wood ash around your parsnips to drive them away.

Parsnips and carrots are susceptible to carrot flies and shouldn't be planted together because it becomes more likely carrot flies will find them. Avoid planting parsnips and other members of the carrot family in the same location in the garden in successive years.

Plant parsnips with other root vegetables or with peppers, radishes or peas.

Good Neighbors:
Garlic, fruit trees, peas, peppers, potatoes, radishes.

Bad Neighbors:
Carrots, onions.

Known Benefits:
Parsnips will attract predatory insects if allowed to go to seed. The roots of the parsnip plant contains a natural

pesticide that's toxic to fruit flies and a handful of other pests.

Peas

The hardest part about growing peas is choosing the variety you want to grow. There are **vining peas** that need to be trellised and **bush peas** that grow close to the ground. There are varieties that are ready for early harvest, normal harvest and late-season harvest. There are wrinkle-seeded and smooth-seeded peas and there are peas that have to be shelled before consumption and peas that you can eat while in the pods.

Early season crops appreciate a bit of protection from cold winds, so plan accordingly. Mid- and late-season peas will do best around taller crops that provide protection from the late afternoon sun.

Peas are bad neighbors to cauliflower because they'll stunt the growth of the cauliflower. Allium family plants like leeks and onions are also bad neighbors to peas because they'll stunt their growth.

Peas are good neighbors to grapes, blackberries, turnips and celery because they add nitrogen to the soil and help them meet their nutritional needs. Cucumbers can be succession planted after peas and can use the same trellis. Snip your pea plants off at the base once production starts to slow and plant cucumbers nearby. They'll benefit from the nitrogen the peas release into the soil. Carrots also work well as a succession crop.

Potatoes and peas can be planted together and will mutually benefit one another. The potatoes will enjoy the nitrogen the peas fix into the soil, while the peas will grow faster.

Good Neighbors:

Asparagus, most Brassica family plants, blackberries, carrots, celery, coriander, corn, cucumbers, grapes, mustard, parsnips, potatoes, radishes, strawberries, turnips.

Bad Neighbors:

Beans, cauliflower, chives, garlic, leeks, onions, parsnips, pole beans, rhubarb, shallots.

Known Benefits:

Peas leave large amounts of nitrogen behind in the soil. They also repel the Colorado potato beetle.

Peppers

From sweet peppers to hot peppers and everything in-between, peppers are generally an easy crop to grow. Give them full sun and well-drained soil rich in organic material and they'll really take off. Peppers require a moderate amount of water. Keep watering consistent, but don't oversaturate the soil. Pepper plants can grow large and may have a lot of heavy peppers on them, so stake the plants while they're young to prevent them from collapsing under their own weight.

Peppers prefer high humidity, so plants that provide ground cover or have dense foliage make good neighbors. Both basil and oregano can be planted to provide ground cover around peppers. Chamomile improves the yield of pepper plants and carrots and onions are said to improve the flavor of both hot and sweet peppers alike.

Don't plant peppers near apricots because the peppers can harbor a fungus that can do a lot of damage to apricots. Eggplant can harbor insects that attack peppers and should be avoided.

Hot peppers release a chemical into the soil that prevents root rot and a handful of other diseases. Planting them near squash, tomatoes and cucumbers will benefit those plants. Peppers and basil are mutually beneficial and both plants see improvement when planted close together. Geraniums and marigolds deter pests that attack peppers and lure in pollinators. Onions, garlic and chives also deter pests known to attack peppers. Rosemary benefits hot peppers and is said to help them grow.

Good Neighbors:

Basil, carrots, chamomile, chives, cucumbers, garlic, geraniums, marigolds, oregano, onions, parsnips, rosemary, squash, sunflowers, tomatoes.

Bad Neighbors:
Apricots, Brassica family members, dill, eggplant, kale, fennel, strawberries.

Known Benefits:
Peppers grow tall and can be used to provide shade to smaller plants. Hot peppers release chemicals into the soil that can prevent root diseases.

Pole Beans

Pole beans are bean plants that need room to grow. They're typically trellised, so they can grow upwards instead spreading out in all directions across the ground. Unlike bush beans, which are harvested over the course of a couple weeks, pole beans will continue producing beans throughout the growing season as long as you continue harvesting them.

Potatoes and summer savory can be planted beneath pole beans to prevent bean beetles from attacking the beans. If you're having problems with aphids, chamomile can be used to attract hover flies that consume aphids. Rhubarb can be planted repel black flies.

Pole beans can be used to provide shade to smaller plants that are sensitive to the afternoon sun. Plant them in a position where they'll provide shade in the afternoon, as opposed to the morning. Lettuce and spinach both will benefit from protection from the sun in warmer climates.

Don't plant sunflowers around pole beans. The roots of the sunflower plant emits a chemical that can slow or even stop the growth of pole beans.

Good Neighbors:

Anise, blackberries, cantaloupe, carrots, chamomile, coriander, corn, eggplant, grains, grapes, lettuce, marigolds, mustard, potatoes, pumpkins, radishes, rhubarb, rosemary, spinach, strawberries, summer savory.

Bad Neighbors:

Beets, Brussels sprouts, bush beans, chives, cucumbers, garlic, fennel, kohlrabi, leeks, onions, peas, sunflowers.

Known Benefits:

Bean plants pull nitrogen from the air and add it to the soil they're grown in. This will benefit plants that need a lot of nitrogen like blackberries, corn and grains that are planted in succession to beans.

Potatoes

Growing potatoes requires a bit of extra effort because the plants must be hilled to ensure potatoes that grow near the surface stay beneath the soil. Potatoes that are exposed to sunlight will turn green and taste bitter, so it's important to make sure this doesn't happen. As potatoes grow, more soil must be pushed up around the potatoes to make sure they stay covered. Potatoes are cool-season crops that require fertile, loose soil. Rotate potato crops on a 3-year cycle where you don't plant potatoes in the same place in the garden until 3 years have passed.

Potatoes shouldn't be planted near apricots because they can spread a disease to apricot trees that stunts growth and negatively impacts harvest. Tomatoes should be avoided as a companion plant, as they can make potatoes more susceptible to root blight. Planting potatoes near cucumbers or sunflowers can stunt their growth. Eggplant doesn't make a good neighbor to potatoes because it attracts insects that are detrimental to potatoes.

Chives or thyme can be planted close to potatoes to aid their growth. Garlic can be used to help prevent potato blight.

Potatoes are susceptible to a number of pests. Buckwheat and marigolds can be planted nearby to eliminate at least some of the pests that attack potatoes. Nasturtiums will repel pests including the Colorado potato beetle, and can be used as a trap crop for aphids. Potatoes can be planted near bush beans to repel bean beetles.

Good Neighbors:

Broccoli, buckwheat, bush beans, cabbage, chives, garlic, kale, marigolds, nasturtiums, parsnips, peas, pole beans, thyme.

Bad Neighbors:

Apricots, asparagus, cantaloupe, carrots, cucumbers, dill, eggplant, pumpkins, raspberries, squash, strawberries, sunflowers, tomatoes.

Known Benefits:

Potatoes repel bean beetles, which is beneficial to both bush beans and pole beans.

Pumpkins

As long as you've got plenty of space in your garden, pumpkins are easy to grow. When planting pumpkins, keep in mind the vines can reach 30' in length and plan accordingly. They can be trained to grow in whatever direction you'd like, so you don't have to provide a 30' radius around your pumpkin plants. Pumpkins need lots of moisture and lots of sun in order to thrive. Try to limit pumpkins to 3 to 4 pumpkins per vine, so the plants are able to provide them the nutrients they need. Additional flowers can be harvested and added to salads.

Pumpkins can be planted in close proximity to corn and beans in a trifecta known as the Three Sisters that benefits all three plants. The beans provide nitrogen by fixing it into the soil and are able to use the corn as a trellis. The pumpkins provide ground cover, keeping weeds away and helping the soil retain moisture. Miniature pumpkins can even be trained to grow up corn stalks as they mature.

Good Neighbors:
Beans, buckwheat, clover, corn, marigolds.

Bad Neighbors:
Potatoes.

Known Benefits:
Pumpkin vines can be trained to grow along rows of other plants, providing ground cover without sucking up nutrients.

Radishes

If you're looking for a quick crop that matures in a matter of weeks, radishes may fit the bill. Some radish varieties are ready for harvest within three weeks of planting. This hardy cool-season crop can be grown in both the spring and the fall and you may be able to get away with growing multiple crops in succession if you live in a mild climate.

Growing lettuce and radishes in close proximity to one another makes radishes tender.

Radishes can be allowed to go to seed to provide cucumbers protection from the cucumber beetle. This effect is only works when the radishes are in bloom. Cucumbers reciprocate by improving the growth rate of radishes. Radishes grown with carrots will loosen up the soil, making it easier for the carrots to send down their roots.

Use radishes as a trap crop to call in flea beetles and other insects that eat leaves. The insects will consume the radish leaves, leaving the root intact. This works well with lettuce and spinach and may be beneficial with other leafy greens.

Good Neighbors:
Cantaloupe, carrots, cucumbers, eggplant, lettuce, nasturtiums, parsnips, peas, pole beans, spinach, squash, watermelons.

Bad Neighbors:
Brassica family plants, grapes, hyssop, kale.

Known Benefits:

Repels aphids, cabbage worms and squash bugs. Let radishes go to seed to repel the cucumber beetle.

Raspberries

Grow a raspberry bush or two and you'll have a perennial plant that'll provide berries for many years to come. Raspberry bushes are low-maintenance additions to the garden that will live for many, many years. Summer-bearing raspberry cultivars provide one berry crop per season, while ever-bearing bushes will provide multiple crops. New bushes won't start providing berries until the second year they've been in the ground.

Raspberries prefer acidic soil and can be grown alongside blueberries, cranberries and rhubarb. Avoid planting raspberries near established wild berry bushes in your garden because they can pick diseases up and spread them to the rest of the garden. Raspberries can catch blight from soil that eggplants, tomatoes and strawberries have been planted in, so wait at least 3 years before planting raspberries in succession to one of these crops.

Japanese beetles will occasionally attack raspberries, so plant garlic nearby to prevent this from happening. Tansy is another good plant to grow near raspberries in order to deter insects. In areas where Harlequin beetles are a problem, turnips and yarrow can be planted to deter these beetles.

Good Neighbors:
Blueberries, bush beans, cranberries, garlic, rhubarb, rue, tansy, turnips, yarrow.

Bad Neighbors:
Eggplant, potatoes, strawberries, tomatoes, wild berry plants.

Known Benefits:
No known benefits.

Rhubarb

The vividly-colored, tart stems of the rhubarb plant can add a touch of color to an otherwise bland garden. Rhubarb grows best in areas where the ground freezes in the winter, as the plants have to experience an extended period of cold before they'll develop edible stalks. Once established, rhubarb is a perennial plant that will continue to provide harvestable stems for up to 10 years. Whatever you do, don't harvest the leaves. They contain oxalic acid and are toxic when ingested.

Rhubarb tolerates acidic soil and can be grown alongside blueberries, cranberries and raspberries. Plant rhubarb alongside beans to repel black flies. Chives are also beneficial to rhubarb. Brassica family plants do well when rhubarb is nearby.

Avoid planting rhubarb around peas because rhubarb has been known to attract the tarnished plant bug.

Good Neighbors:
Beans, blueberries, Brassica family plants, cranberries, chives, raspberries.

Bad Neighbors:
Peas.

Known Benefits:
Rhubarb repels black flies.

Rosemary

Rosemary is a perennial plant that can be grown as an evergreen hedge in warmer climates. In cooler climates, it can be grown in containers that can be brought inside when the weather turns cold. Rosemary prefers full sun, but can be grown successfully in partial shade. Rosemary can be harvested any time after it's established. Trim a stem or two off the plant and hang it to dry.

Planting rosemary near broccoli, Brussels sprouts, cabbage, beans or peppers will help both plants reach their full potential.

Good Neighbors:
Beans, broccoli, Brussels sprouts, cabbage, nettles, peppers, turnips.

Bad Neighbors:
Carrots.

Known Benefits:
Repels carrot flies, cabbage moths and Mexican bean beetles. Also repels the flies that lay eggs that turn into root maggots.

Roses

Grow roses in full sun for best results. Roses that don't get at least 4 to 6 hours of sun a day are more susceptible to powdery mildew and fungal diseases. There are a small handful of cultivars that can tolerate partial shade, but they do better in full sun.

Roses are particularly susceptible to insect attack. Chamomile and marigolds can be planted nearby to call in hoverflies that will make short work of the aphids. Mint and onions drive away aphids and other insects that attack roses. Chives can be planted near roses to help prevent black spot. Geraniums can be planted near roses to repel cabbage worms and beetles. Basil and garlic can also be planted nearby to repel pests.

Plant parsley below your rose bushes to improve the scent of the roses and to deter the rose beetle.

Good Neighbors:
Basil, chamomile, chives, garlic, geraniums, lavender, marigolds, mint, onions, parsley, rue, tansy.

Bad Neighbors:
No known bad neighbors.

Known Benefits:
No known benefits.

Rue

Rue is a drought-resistant perennial herb that enjoys hot, dry climates and can be grown in soil that's of poor quality. If you've got an area near your garden where you're having trouble getting plants to grow, there's a pretty good chance rue can be grown there. Just don't plant it too close to your house. Rue has a strong smell most people find unpleasant.

Be aware the oils of the rue plant can cause an allergic reaction known as **photodermatitis** when they come in contact with the skin. The oil gets on your skin and then reacts with sunlight, causing blistering or a rash. Always wear gloves and protective clothing when handling this potent little plant.

Basil and rue shouldn't be planted close together, as they'll inhibit one another's growth. Rue is typically planted near raspberries or roses to repel insects that commonly attack those plants.

Good Neighbors:
Raspberries, roses, strawberries.

Bad Neighbors:
Anise, basil, cauliflower.

Known Benefits:
Repels cucumber beetles, flea beetles, Japanese beetles, fleas and white flies.

Sage

The gray-green foliage of sage really stands out in most gardens. This perennial shrub grows wider than it is tall and is as comfortable being grown in a container as it is in the ground. Sage doesn't tolerate heat and humidity, so it may not make it through a hot summer if it isn't potted and brought indoors during the heat of the day. Swap out sage plants after 3 years, as older plants don't produce the same quality of sage as younger plants do.

Sage can stunt the growth of cucumbers. It is said to enhance the growth of broccoli, Brussels sprouts, cabbage, carrots, strawberries and tomatoes.

Good Neighbors:
Broccoli, Brussels sprouts, cabbage, carrots, cauliflower, nettles, strawberries, tomatoes, turnips.

Bad Neighbors:
Basil, cucumbers, garlic, onions, rue.

Known Benefits:
Repels cabbage worms, carrot flies, root maggots and caterpillars. Attracts honeybees and other pollinators.

Spinach

Grow spinach as a cool weather crop because warm weather will cause it to bolt, at which time it becomes bitter and sends up a seed stalk. Spinach plants send a taproot deep into the soil in search of nutrients, so make sure the soil you plant it in is loose.

Spinach may be able to be grown in warmer weather if it's shaded from the afternoon sun. Tall companion plants like tomatoes, pole beans and corn can be used to shade spinach and prolong the growing season. Planting spinach together with cauliflower has been shown to benefit both plants. Alternate rows of spinach with rows of cauliflower for best results.

Good Neighbors:
Broccoli, cauliflower, chives, coriander, corn, eggplants, pole beans, radishes, tomatoes.

Bad Neighbors:
No known bad neighbors.

Known Benefits:
No known benefits.

Squash

There are two basic types of squash. **Summer squash**, which includes zucchini, are harvested while immature and the skins are edible. **Winter squash** are vining squash plants that are allowed to grow until fall arrives. These squash are allowed to grow until mature and have thicker, tougher skin that has to be removed before eating. Growing squash in areas with extreme hot or cold temperatures is difficult because squash is susceptible to both frost and heat damage.

Squash is an aggressive grower and will compete with smaller plants for light and nutrients. Plants with a small stature like beets will suffer when planted close to squash.

Catnip repels aphids, which is beneficial to squash. Chives are also known to benefit squash. Hot peppers are a good companion plant for squash because they release chemicals into the soil that combats root rot and other diseases.

Borage is a good neighbor to squash because it attracts pollinators. Nasturtiums are beneficial because they will draw aphids away from squash and are thought to improve the flavor of squash when planted nearby. Radishes can be used as a trap crop to lure flea beetles away and marigolds can be used to deter squash bugs and cucumber beetles.

Good Neighbors:
Borage, buckwheat, catnip, chives, corn, hot peppers, lavender, lemon balm, marigolds, nasturtiums, radishes, sunflowers, tomatoes.

Bad Neighbors:

Beets, cucumbers, potatoes.

Known Benefits:
No known benefits.

Stinging Nettles

Stinging nettle plants grow wild across much of North America. They can grow pretty much anywhere, propagate rapidly and are known to spread in a manner similar to mint. Wear gloves when handling stinging nettles, as they produce a chemical that can irritate the skin. This chemical is rendered inactive when stinging nettles are cooked and they can be used to make tea or eaten as steamed greens.

Nettles are said to increase the length of time produce is able to be kept after it's harvested. This is especially beneficial to fruits like tomatoes. Nettles are also beneficial to aromatic herbs like mint and basil because they increase essential oil production in the herbs when planted nearby.

Good Neighbors:
Aromatic herbs, tomatoes.

Bad Neighbors:
No known bad neighbors.

Known Benefits:
Nettles are said to improve the flavor of a number of plants and may provide protection against disease. Nettles repel aphids.

Strawberries

There are three basic types of strawberry plants to select from. **Everbearing** and **day neutral strawberries** produce fruit throughout the year, while **June bearing strawberries** produce a single crop at the end of spring. Strawberries prefer full sun and do well when planted in well-drained, loamy soil.

Strawberries can be difficult to grow and are subject to a variety of pests and diseases. They attract slugs that will prey on low-lying plants, so avoid planting them near leafy greens. Lettuce is the exception to this rule and generally does well when planted near strawberries.

They're subject to verticillium rot and shouldn't be planted in areas where tomatoes, peppers or potatoes have recently been planted. Flowering herbs with strong scents like borage, catnip, rue, basil, yarrow and chamomile are of strawberries by preventing insect good neighbors to strawberries because they attract pollinators and drive away some pests. Buckwheat is also said to be a good neighbor to strawberries and sage is said to enhance their growth. Beans and peas add nitrogen to the soil that can be used by strawberries. Thyme is said to aid the growth of strawberries and calls in pollinators.

Strawberries can be planted to provide ground cover to the exposed stems of blackberries, which in turn provide light shade to the strawberries, keeping them cool in the heat of the summer. Blueberries and cranberries also benefit from having strawberries planted nearby.

Good Neighbors:

Asparagus, basil, beans, blackberries, blueberries, borage, buckwheat, catnip, chamomile, cranberries, leeks, lettuce, onions, peas, rue, sage, thyme.

Bad Neighbors:
Broccoli, Brussels sprouts, cabbage, cauliflower, kale, leafy greens, peppers, potatoes, raspberries, tomatoes.

Known Benefits:
Strawberries spread out and choke out weed growth in areas where they're planted. This benefits thin plants like asparagus.

Sunflowers

Sunflowers live up to their name, as they prefer open areas with plenty of sunlight. As long as they get the light they need, sunflowers can be grown in pretty much any soil, as evidenced by the fact they can be seen growing wild alongside roads across the United States. They grow tall and can be planted to provide shade to plants like lettuce that are susceptible to the heat of the afternoon sun.

Soybeans and mustard are considered bad neighbors to sunflowers because they share common diseases and can pass them amongst each other.

Keep sunflowers away from pole beans and potatoes. The roots of sunflowers emit a chemical that will stop the beans and potatoes from growing. This effect is more pronounced with wild sunflowers than it is with cultivated sunflowers.

Good Neighbors:
Corn, cucumbers, lettuce, peppers, squash, tomatoes.

Bad Neighbors:
Beets, mustard, pole beans, potatoes, soybeans.

Known Benefits:
Sunflowers draw in pollinators and ladybugs that will feed on soft-shelled insects. Can be used as a trap plant for aphids and thrips.

Tansy

Tansy has fern-like foliage and yellow flowers that look great in a planter or dispersed amongst the fruit and vegetables growing in your garden. This hardy perennial requires full sun and is drought-tolerant. Exercise caution when considering where to plant tansy. It's highly toxic to humans and many animals and can make kids, pets and livestock sick if they happen to graze on it.

If you're having pest problems, there's a good chance tansy can help. It repels a number of pest insects, while calling in even more predatory insects. Tansy can benefit most plants, but corn, cucumbers, beans, roses and raspberries benefit most. If you want to enhance the growth of your tansy plants, grow cabbage nearby.

Good Neighbors:
Beans, cabbage, cantaloupe, corn, cucumbers, fruit trees, mustard, raspberries, roses.

Bad Neighbors:
No known bad neighbors.

Known Benefits:
Tansy repels ants, beetles and flying insects. It calls in pirate bugs, ladybugs, tachinid flies, lacewings and parasitic wasps. Tansy also adds potassium to the soil.

Thyme

Thyme is an aromatic perennial herb featuring a scent that's pleasant to humans, but a number of bugs detest it. Thyme prefers full sun and slightly alkaline, well-drained soil. It's equally comfortable planted in containers or sowed directly into the soil.

Plant thyme with tomatoes to improve the taste of the tomatoes. Cabbage, eggplant and strawberries also benefit from having thyme nearby.

Good Neighbors:

Brussels sprouts, cabbage, eggplants, strawberries, tomatoes.

Bad Neighbors:
Eggplant.

Known Benefits:

Thyme repels cabbage worms, corn earworms, tomato hornworms and flea beetles. It attracts hoverflies, honeybees and other pollinators.

Tomatoes

Tomatoes are one of the most popular crops in the United States. There are cultivars available for most areas. Make sure their water needs are met and they're planted in fertile soil and they're fairly easy to grow.

Avoid planting tomatoes near broccoli and cauliflower crops because the tomatoes will suck up much of the nutrients in the soil, thereby slowing the growth of the cauliflower. Tomatoes shouldn't be planted near apricots because they can pass diseases to the apricot trees or near eggplants because they draw in pests that will attack tomatoes. Brassica oleracea family members and dill can inhibit the growth of tomatoes, so make sure you plant them on opposite ends of the garden. Fennel also stunts the growth of tomatoes.

Tomatoes and young dill plants are good companions, but mature dill plants will begin competing with tomatoes for nutrients.

Try planting basil and tomatoes close to one another. Both plants may end up tasting better and growing faster as a result. Planting asparagus near tomatoes will help repel the nematodes that attack tomatoes.

Planting carrots near tomatoes will improve the yield of the tomatoes, while lessening the yield of the carrots. Chives have a beneficial effect on tomatoes and don't suffer any ill effects when planted nearby. Sage is another good plant to grow around tomatoes. Nettles are said to increase the length of time tomatoes can be kept after harvest before they start to go bad. Alfalfa, on the other hand, has been shown to be allelopathic when planted around tomato seedlings, so give these two plants a wide berth.

Tomatoes are highly susceptible to aphid attack. Catnip and mint can be planted nearby to help deter aphids. Chamomile attracts hoverflies, a known predator of aphids. In some areas, tomatoes are seemingly under constant siege from tomato hornworms. Borage can be planted nearby to reduce the risk of hornworm attack. Marigolds are another good plant to have around tomatoes, as are plants from the mint family. Corn attracts a worm that's similar to the tomato fruit worm and planting it close to tomatoes could mean more of both worms will show up.

Tomatoes are also susceptible to diseases that affect their roots. Hot peppers can be planted around tomatoes to help combat these diseases. Lettuce can be planted close to tomatoes to provide at least some level of protection to their roots.

Good Neighbors:
Asparagus, basil, borage, carrots, catnip, chamomile, chives, coriander, garlic, hot peppers, lavender, leeks, lemon balm, lettuce, marigolds, mint, nettles, onions, parsley, sage, spinach, squash, sunflowers, thyme.

Bad Neighbors:
Alfalfa, apricots, beets, Brassica family members, bush beans, corn, dill, eggplant, fennel, potatoes, raspberries, strawberries.

Known Benefits:
Tomatoes contain a chemical compound known as *solanine* that drives away pests like the asparagus beetle and cabbage worms.

Turnips

Turnips are a cool weather crop that thrives during the spring and fall in most regions. Once the weather turns too warm, the roots of the turnip plant will turn bitter. Plant turnips in well-drained, loose soil that's deep enough to ensure they'll have room to grow. Consistent watering is the key to unlocking deliciously-flavored turnips. Turnip greens can also be harvested, but make sure you leave some of the leaves attached to the plant to ensure the root is able to finish developing.

Since turnips are from the Brassica family of plants, they shouldn't be planted in the same location as most other Brassica family members in successive years. This will prevent the soil from being stripped of nutrients and will prepare it for future Brassica crops. They can be used as a trap crop to lure pests away from other Brassica crops.

Peas are a good companion for turnips because of the nitrogen they add to the soil. Both turnips and peas are cool weather crops that have similar requirements.

Root maggots are a common pest that plagues turnips. Aromatic herbs like dill, sage and rosemary will deter the adult flies that lay the eggs that turn into the maggots. Celery can also be planted to repel flies.

Good Neighbors:
Broccoli, cauliflower, celery, dill, peas, sage, raspberries, rosemary.

Bad Neighbors:
Pole beans, potatoes.

Known Benefits:
Deters the Harlequin beetle.

Watermelons

To grow watermelons, you're going to need warm days, a long growing season, consistent watering and well-drained, fertile soil. Make sure the last frost has passed before planting watermelon seedlings because they're extremely sensitive to cold. Watermelon plants require quite a bit of room to spread out. If you don't have a lot of room, you may be able to build a trellis, but you're going to need a sturdy one.

Watermelon is a strong grower and can crowd out smaller plants like beets and carrots. Radishes, marigolds and nasturtiums can be planted alongside watermelons to repel pests. They serve double-duty by attracting pollinators to help pollinate the watermelons once they bloom and can be used as a trap crop to keep aphids away from more desirable plants.

Avoid planting citron melons near watermelons. They can cross-pollinate the watermelons and things can get a bit unpredictable. Keep cucumbers away from watermelons as well because they attract cucumber beetles that love to dine on watermelon. The worst companion for watermelon plants is other watermelon plants. Plant them too close together and they'll smother one another while competing for resources.

Watermelon is one of the few plants capable of growing around a black walnut tree, but just because it's capable, doesn't mean you should. The plants will often suffer reduced yields and stunted growth.

Good Neighbors:
Corn, marigolds, nasturtiums, radishes.

Bad Neighbors:
Beets, broccoli, carrots, citron melons, cucumbers, lemon balm.

Known Benefits:
No known benefits, other than providing shade and ground cover.

Walnuts, Black

Black walnut trees aren't good neighbors to most plants and trees because the roots of trees release a chemical known as **juglone** that causes nearby plants to turn yellow and die off. According to the University of Wisconsin, black walnut trees can extend their toxicity as far as 80' feet away from the trunk. This is great for the walnut tree because it isn't going to have much competition, but it can be a real hassle for the gardener unlucky enough to have one nearby.

Further compounding this problem is the fact that a variety of other trees are grown on black walnut rootstock.
If you have a tree that you're having trouble growing companion plants around that isn't black walnut, there's a possibility black walnut rootstock was used.

Good Neighbors:
Very few plants can be grown around black walnuts.

Bad Neighbors:
Most plants and trees.

Known Benefits:
None.

Additional Reading

If you enjoyed this book, you might enjoy the following book about survival seeds and heirloom gardening:

http://www.amazon.com/Survival-Seeds-Heirloom-Saving-Handbook-ebook/dp/B00J2I0416/

Made in the USA
San Bernardino, CA
11 April 2020